Ray Connolly has been writing about popular music for more than fifteen years. After working as a journalist in Liverpool, in 1967 he joined the London *Evening Standard* as a columnist and writer on rock music. During this time he was very involved in the daily affairs of the Beatles and wrote many articles on John Lennon, Yoko Ono and Paul McCartney.

In 1973 he wrote his first film, *That'll Be the Day*, which starred Ringo Starr. His second film, a year later, was *Stardust*, an account of an English rock group which took America by storm in the sixties. *Stardust* won him the Writers Guild of Great Britain Award for the best original screenplay. He is also the author of seven novels and nine television plays, and has written and directed an eighty-minute film documentary on James Dean.

Ray Connolly, who is forty, was educated in Lancashire and then at the London School of Economics where he read social anthropology. He is married, has three children and lives in London. He is a regular contributor to the *Sunday Times* and the *New Standard*.

John Lennon
1940–1980

Ray Connolly

FONTANA PAPERBACKS

First published by Fontana Paperbacks 1981
Copyright © Ray Connolly 1981

Set in Lasercomp Times
Made and printed in Great Britain by
William Collins Sons & Co. Ltd, Glasgow

For Jane

'Have you written my obituary yet? I'd
love to read it when you do.'

John Lennon to Ray Connolly,
December 1970.

Contents

Acknowledgments

Much of this book draws on articles I wrote for the *New Standard* (then the *Evening Standard*) in the sixties and seventies. I am grateful to that newspaper for the opportunity it gave me to come so close to the Beatles during those years, and for permission to make use of the material I wrote then.

For permission to reproduce photographs I and the publishers are grateful to the following: Associated Press (7, 14, 18, 19, 28, 39 *above*, 49); Tom Hanley (16, 37); Keystone Press (4, 5 *below*, 6, 9, 11, 12, 20, 22, 25, 29, 31, 34 *below*, 35, 41, 42, 43, 44, 47, 48, 50, 51, 53 *below*); London Features International (27, 32 *above*, 33); Popperfoto (2, 3, 5 *above*, 8, 10, 13, 15, 17, 21, 23, 24, 26, 32 *below*, 34 *above*, 36, 39 *below*, 40, 45, 46, 52, 53 *above*); Rex Features (1, 30, 38).

My thanks are also due to John Spencer who found all the photographs.

With the exception of the songs quoted from *Walls and Bridges* and *Double Fantasy*, published respectively by Lennon Music ATV Music Ltd and Lenono Music Ltd, all the quoted songs are published by Northern Songs Ltd.

The drawings of John, Yoko and Sean Lennon are reproduced from a letter John wrote to me in 1976. His letters were often signed in this way.

Finally, I'd like to thank Sally Baker who stayed up into the small hours typing the manuscript.

Foreword

At exactly three thirty on the afternoon of Monday, 8 December 1980, the telephone in the room in which I work in London's Holland Park rang. It was Yoko Ono calling from New York.

'Hey, Ray, when are you going to come and do this interview with John and me?' she asked.

'What about tomorrow?' I suggested.

'That's great. The sooner the better,' she replied, and after a few social pleasantries and promises to meet the next day we hung up. It had taken us six weeks to agree on a date.

At five thirty the following morning the telephone rang in my bedroom. My first thought was that it was Yoko calling to tell me that there had been some hitch in the arrangements and advising me to cancel my trip to the States. It was, in fact, a friend from the *Daily Mail* in Fleet Street.

'Ray . . . we've had a report in that John Lennon has been shot. I thought you ought to know,' he said.

I went downstairs and turned on the radio and waited for the confirmation. At six thirty I began writing the obituary I had promised to show him ten years earlier.

John Lennon was the chameleon of rock music. He was everything to everyone. He was the rebel, the rocker, the working-class hero; the grammar school boy who thought he was a genius but who didn't pass a single GCE 'O' level; the psychedelic Walrus of legend who once admitted to taking literally 'thousands' of acid trips; the vicious wit who could wound with a word; the ever-generous supporter of causes – lost, worthy, dubious, or whatever; the massive tipper, the media freak; the obsessive self-publicist; the retiring, reclusive hermit; the wild man of Hamburg; the bed man of peace; the Egg Man of *Magical Mystery Tour* and the Nowhere Man of a mansion in the stockbroker belt.

John Lennon lived for nearly half his life under the constant, often admiring, sometimes derisive gaze of media glare. It was as he chose it to be. As a child he once considered the idea of being a journalist because he 'wanted to be a writer, and journalism was the only kind of writing that people from my background could aspire to'. Later he became obsessed with news coverage, and with the manipulation of that coverage to his own ends.

Very early in his career as a Beatle he learned how the press could be charmed into providing massive free publicity, and he rarely missed a chance of self-promotion when it could prove useful. He was friendly to journalists and understood very well their role and the difficulties in their chosen profession. And he rarely failed to speak in the most quotable of sentences, tossing out outrageous comments, knowing as if by instinct the art of speaking in headlines. He may not have realized quite what he was starting when he told Maureen Cleave that the Beatles were 'more popular than Jesus' in 1966 (possibly one of the most obvious truisms of the decade), but by 1969, when he was joking to reporters about being down to his last £50,000, he could already see the headlines of the next day's tabloid newspapers.

Between 1967 and 1972 I was in the position of being on the receiving end of all kinds of headline-grabbing Lennon stories when I was covering the Beatles and all things allied for the London *Evening Standard*. Although for a few years John and Yoko showed me great friendship and kindness, I could never be unaware that to them a great deal of my attraction lay in my value as a sympathetic ear in Fleet Street. When John married secretly in Gibraltar the *Evening Standard* were happy to have an exclusive; when he handed back his MBE it was John who telephoned with the news long before the announcement came from either Apple or Buckingham Palace; and when he decided to leave the Beatles I did as he asked and sat on the story for four months, although it would undoubtedly have been the best news story I could have ever hoped to run in my days as a reporter. (That was a miscalculation on both our parts. I missed the exclusive of a lifetime, and John cursed himself for allowing Paul the dubious prestige of being the man to tell the world that the Beatles were finished, an unhappy irony for Paul since he was the one Beatle who had tried hardest and longest to keep their singing comradeship afloat.)

This book is not intended to be an 'I was there' account of John Lennon's career – mainly because for much of it I was not there. When the Lennons moved to America in 1971 we kept in vague touch with each other, exchanging the occasional jokey letter, but between 1976 and 1980 I, like most journalists, lost touch with them completely. I have, therefore, had to rely to some extent upon the work of other journalists, and upon the memories of the principal characters and their accounts of their lives as told to me and to other writers. Wherever possible I have, however, used first-hand knowledge and accounts. Wherever I have used quotations made to other writers I have tried to be quite sure that they are accurate, and wherever possible to credit the source of the quotation. This, however, is not always possible because, like everyone else, John Lennon tended to say the same things in slightly different ways to many different people. Thus when the famous *Rolling Stone* interviews (issued in the UK as *Lennon Remembers* by Penguin Books) were first published, many of us who had been around him at that time found that we were not reading anything particularly new.

The other thing which must be borne in mind is that memory colours everything, and John Lennon was as prone to seeing things through his own particular viewpoint as anyone else. Thus, during the vexed period of the break-up of the Beatles I have tried to give Paul McCartney's version of events as much credence as John Lennon's, because I am sure they are equally valid.

This book is not a tribute, it is a biography: a biography about a man I knew well for several years, and whose career I followed for nearly twenty years. It is about a man who reflected the changing times, and who, on occasion, may even have helped shape those changes. It is not a book about a saint, but about someone who wrote and played rock and roll music better than virtually anyone else. Norman Mailer said that John Lennon had a genius of spirit. That was true, but there was something else. When he died, millions of people mourned the loss of a friend. His real genius was in his ability to communicate. He was to perfection a creature of his times.

John Lennon was more than just a hero of rock and roll whose tragic flaw, a lifelong ambition to be rich and famous, was to lead to his murder in the courtyard of his New York castle home. He was not an Elvis Presley who was 'killed by his courtiers' while numbed to the world outside him. John Lennon was always part of the world around him; it fed him, and he illustrated it with dazzling imagery and songs which became anthems and nursery rhymes, tapestries of words and melody which recorded, however obliquely, the steps of his lifetime, and our lives.

When I first considered this book my initial feeling was that it should be like a children's pop-up book, one of those beautifully illustrated pageants of history in which the characters stand up three-dimensionally as the pages are opened. That is how I see the life of John Lennon. All the stages of his life have a theatricality: a series of tableaux, if you like, featuring the media heroes of the past four decades.

Aaron Copland once said that when future generations wanted to capture the spirit of the sixties all they would have to do was to play Beatle records. That's true, but I would go further. Future historians will find the understanding of the sixties and the seventies widened immeasurably by focusing on the life of John Lennon. From Liverpool war baby to killer's victim just across the road from Central Park, Lennon's every interest told a story of the times.

The widespread grief at his death was compared with the

mourning which followed the assassination of President Kennedy. No one should have been surprised, although many were. There were some parallels: both were relatively young men murdered by apparently deranged fanatics. Both had been the subject of massive media exposure, and both had appeared to offer visions of idealism. But whereas Kennedy was a shrewd political mover whose publicity was geared towards his own flattery, John Lennon chose the role of anti-hero for much of his life, casting off the trappings of glamour, throwing aside the shell of lovable immortality. John Lennon would never have made a politician. Political heroes are pragmatists. That is their job. John Lennon had no time for pragmatism. He was outspoken about everything and everybody, and then bore the consequences for his outrageousness.

He was a true original. He said what he thought, although it is not always certain that he thought enough about what he said. But that was part of his attraction. He made mistakes, wide open, howling mistakes. And then he had to live with them. He lived his life on his cuff. He was unpredictable. Every few years he would apparently tire of one lifestyle, and, without a backward glance, move on to something else, leaving behind him all the ephemera of previous existences.

When asked what he (and Yoko) expected to be doing when he was sixty-four, a song which, incidentally, Paul McCartney wrote completely, John told *Rolling Stone*: 'I hope we're a nice old couple living off the coast of Ireland or something like that – looking at our scrapbook of madness.'

Sometimes it would seem to me he was like an actor, juggling with the different personalities inside himself, personalities which from time to time would emerge and take him upon a roller coaster ride of frenzied activity, before being replaced by his lifelong habit of daydreaming. He even gave himself new names to go with the characters which existed inside his multi-faceted personality. Sometimes he would be the guru of rock and roll, *Dr Winston O'Boogie*, at others he would be *Johnandor Yoko*. He was a Beatle, but he created another existence inside the Plastic Ono Band. He was christened Winston but he became an Ono.

He was a bewilderment of apparent contradictions. He was English through and through, yet he chose to spend the last quarter of his life living in America. 'It is an Englishman's inalienable right to live wherever he likes,' he would say, misquoting Somerset Maugham. But wherever he went he took his Englishness with him. In the midst of his turbulent Hollywood middle-aged bachelor days, Princess Anne chose to marry. He stayed up to watch the event live on television. 'After all,' he said, with only a slight hint of self-mockery, 'I am an Englishman.'

But it was among Americans that he found greatest affection and freedom. Because he would not conform, the English press turned him into a freak, he felt. Certainly he was always good for a headline. But he was stifled by the attitudes which demanded that he follow a lifestyle for which he no longer cared. He had an extraordinary prescience for picking up on shifts of mood, and a gift for articulating those moods in simple eight-bar chants. When his song 'Give Peace a Chance' was sung by hundreds of thousands of people demonstrating against the Vietnamese War at the Washington Moratorium he was justifiably proud.

It is far too early to sum up the contribution which John Lennon made to our culture. His peace campaign had no tangible results, but through him millions of people were able to articulate their own feelings and worries. He was the medium through which the messages of many were delivered. Sometimes it seemed as though his whole being was like a vacuum cleaner which sucked in all the emotions and popular movements of the moment, and which he would then turn into song.

He was sometimes very silly, but he was never a coward, never a man to duck a confrontation with the narrow-minded. By nature he was a comic, an exhibitionist, who could never resist putting out his tongue at the staid forces of the establishment.

But behind the mockery was a man easily hurt by a careless headline or cruel comment. He was often cruel himself, but he

18

compensated with a massive generosity. He was, he said, guilty at being rich when he had always considered himself a working-class socialist, and to assuage the guilt he gave lavishly to numerous charities, reportedly tithing ten per cent of his income to charity at the end of his life.

That he should have died just at the moment when he had decided to resume his career was a bitter irony. But then his life was a series of ironies. He hated the 'intellectual bullshit' which was written about his records, but it was that intellectualizing which elevated him above the status of all other rock stars. He insisted that he was basically just a rocker, but then went on to write poetic and moving lyrics wrapped inside melodies of tender originality. One of his best songs was written after he heard Yoko playing 'Moonlight Sonata'. 'If you can play those chords backwards I could write a song around that,' he told her. He was opposed to organized religion, and distrustful of the worship of the Beatles by fans, but in his death he became the most deified star of them all.

Dr Winston O'Boogie never had the opportunity to look back on his scrapbook of madness. He would have been fascinated by it.

I

Liverpool

A War Baby in
Strawberry Fields

Forty years ago the city of Liverpool was restless and threatened, a
place of daily insecurity and nightly fears, of black-outs, blitz and
tears, of live-for-the-moment hedonism and lonely months of
waiting. 'Please don't take my sunshine away,' said the words to
one of the most popular of wartime songs, capturing perfectly the
anxiety which haunted families as they waited for the bombing
raids, or huddled in tearful farewells around the blackened, soot-
covered troop trains of Lime Street, and across the vast expanse of
that windswept portside concourse known as the Pier Head. Please
don't take my sunshine away, prayed mothers and wives, while
little children hid inside knitted balaclava helmets and mittens,
frightened of tomorrow, of the dread of evacuation, of being left
behind, and always of being lost in the crowd.

It was into this world of shifting, confused and lonely people
that John Lennon was born at six thirty in the evening of 9 October
1940 at the Oxford Street Maternity Hospital, Liverpool. Outside
a heavy bombing raid was shaking the city. In a spurious moment
of patriotism his mother Julia Lennon gave him the middle name
of Winston. No one knew where his father was. He had gone to
war at sea months earlier. At his birth John Lennon was already
the child of a broken home.

The marriage between Julia Stanley and Freddie Lennon was
never a success. Freddie had himself been an orphan and when he
met and courted John's mother he faced staunch disapproval from
Julia's family, especially her three older sisters. Julia was a flighty,

flippant girl who worked as a cinema usherette. Freddie was totally irresponsible. The couple had been married for less than two years, but because Freddie was a waiter on a ship and spent most of his married life at sea, Julia had stayed at home with her parents, which is where she took her new baby. At first Freddie sent funds for the upkeep of his wife and child but after eighteen months even that stopped. The marriage was finished in everything but name. In adulthood John described his father as 'a drunk and virtually a Bowery bum'.

There was always a slight mystery about the personality of Julia. Certainly she was considered the black sheep of the Stanley family for having married Freddie in the first place, and as a mother to John she was quite unable to cope. But neither John nor any of his aunts ever publicly criticized her. Eventually Julia and Freddie were divorced, she met another man and went to live with him, leaving John, aged three, to be looked after by his favourite aunt, Mary Smith – Auntie Mimi.

Although John later wrote love songs about his mother, he never talked about his two half-sisters who were born in the mid-forties; and, curiously, they never made public their relationship, although at the time of Beatlemania they were the same age as the fans. Later, Auntie Mimi told writer Hunter Davies for his book *The Beatles*: 'I never told John about his father and mother. I just wanted to protect him from all that. Perhaps I was over-anxious. I don't know. I just wanted him to be happy.'

Freddie Lennon resurfaced at the end of the war, having decided to go and live in New Zealand. He took John off to Blackpool for a few weeks, but eventually Julia turned up and John returned to Liverpool with her. The next time John saw Freddie was when he opened a copy of the *Daily Express* at the height of Beatlemania and saw a picture of his father washing dishes in a restaurant.

Back in Liverpool John was returned to Auntie Mimi and her husband, Uncle George. By Liverpool's standards they were a relatively prosperous couple: they lived in their own mock-Tudor semi-detached house in Menlove Avenue, Woolton, which in those days was a nicer suburb of an unlovely city. The legendary Strawberry Fields, a Salvation Army children's home, was just around the corner. Uncle George had his own dairy business. But to say that John Lennon had a middle-class upbringing would be to stretch the definition. 'We had a house with a front and back garden, which was about one step up the scale from Paul and George who lived in council houses,' John would say when asked about this. All the same he was never the street urchin of mythology, certainly not until he left the maternal care and attention of Mimi when he was eighteen. Mimi may not have been his mother, but she behaved towards him as though he were her own child. It was not by chance that John later defied his public image so often by displaying the best of social behaviour. When it suited him he could be courteous and well mannered, unlike the three other Beatles who could be downright boorish. John may not always have behaved well (indeed in his youth he did not often behave well), but he always knew how to should needs arise.

John's first school was the local Dovedale Primary where he was noticed as being bright and quick with words, but of independent spirit. At the age of seven he began writing his own little books, which contained jokes, small drawings, stories and pasted-in photographs of film stars and footballers. With a proper sense of his own importance he would write 'Edited and Illustrated by J. W. Lennon'. Remembering his childhood later he would say: 'I used to think that I was either a genius or a madman, and since I didn't think I was mad I decided I must be a genius.' He was certainly an early and avid reader, his favourite books being *Alice in Wonderland, The Wind in the Willows* and the *Just William* series by Richmal Crompton, stories of a naughty, but very funny small boy. John undoubtedly cast himself in William's image, as did so many other boys at that time.

Although Julia had turned her son over to Mimi she did visit him occasionally, singing him songs and joking with him. One of the songs she sang was from a Walt Disney cartoon, which John later turned into one of his first songs – 'Listen, do you want to know a secret, do you promise not to tell'.

When John wasn't reading or drawing he would listen to the radio. Mimi was not interested in popular music and so the radio in their house would usually be tuned to the BBC Home Service, which presented the excellent *Children's Hour*, the news and the best in radio comedy. Those were the great days of radio in Britain, and a child could get a quite comprehensive education from listening intelligently to the BBC. John Lennon did. Years later he would laugh about comedy shows with which he had grown up, comedians like Nat Jackley and duos like Jimmy Jewel and Ben Warris in *Up the Pole*.

Although in many ways John was a precocious child, he was also tough and aggressive, and parents would warn their children to stay away from him. He was a natural leader and always wanted the other children to play his games, in which he could be the boss. He usually won any arguments by virtue of his menacing behaviour. At home he was the quiet, sensitive child, always singing and leaving flattering notes for his Uncle George (he never got out of the habit of writing people little notes), but in the streets he was the naughty boy of the neighbourhood, trying to pull down girls' knickers, shoplifting, playing truant, and even on one occasion trying unsuccessfully to derail a tram in nearby Penny Lane.

But it was always childhood naughtiness rather than real delinquency. For some reason he found a need to act tough. Later he would say that he was always delicate and sensitive inside, but his early teachers were rarely treated to that side of his nature. His best friends at primary school were Pete Shotton and Ivan Vaughan, and they remained his friends for most of his life.

At the age of eleven one of those strange quirks of fortune occurred which, several years later, was to help change the course of popular music. All three friends passed the eleven-plus examination which meant that they could go on to grammar school. John and Pete were sent to a local suburban school, Quarry Bank High School. Ivan went to the more respected Liverpool Institute in the centre of the city. It was at the Institute that Ivan eventually met Paul McCartney, and it was Ivan who eventually took Paul along to meet John.

The fifties provided opportunities for the achievers in English education. The 1944 Education Act had assured that brighter children who reached a certain level of competence at the age of eleven should be offered free secondary education until the age of sixteen, and be granted financial help, depending on intelligence, merit and hard work, through university. For better or worse the system creamed off the children who showed ability, encouraging academic goals, and it was considered by many something of a privilege for a working-class child to be given such an opportunity to better himself entirely at the ratepayers' expense. Many of the grammar school children of the fifties were aware that they had been given this one chance in life, and that they had better make sure they made the most of it.

But if John Lennon recognized any of this he never showed it. His academic career was disastrous. The only public examination he ever passed was the scholarship which took him to Quarry Bank, an old-fashioned grammar school where masters aped their public school counterparts and wore gowns. He was undoubtedly a child of some considerable ability, but there was equally no doubt that he had absolutely no interest in the educational system, and spent most of his time being the clown of the form. What probably made his teachers increasingly irate was that he was always the smart Alec, always the ring-leader for trouble. He had been resentful towards Mimi for not taking his poetry seriously, and now he was resentful towards his school for not recognizing the genius he thought he was. In those days the only way a child could show ability was in the quality of his work and facility for passing examinations. John was articulate and witty, and obviously had a talent for art and English, but none of that ever showed in his school reports. Teachers complained that he wasted not only his own time, but also that of the rest of the form. He was a leader in childish anarchy.

His wit, however, was not entirely ignored or unappreciated. While his teachers would show disgust when they confiscated his obscene drawings and rhyming couplets, the magazine he scribbled into an exercise book, and which he christened the *Daily Howl*, was more appreciated in the staffroom, with its goonish weather forecast – 'Tomorrow will be Muggy, followed by Tuggy, Wuggy and Thuggy' – and satire on Davy Crockett, 'The Story of Davy Crutch-Head'.

When he was nearly thirteen Mimi's husband died. Uncle George was the closest male relative John had ever had, but the blow was probably cushioned by the increasing interest that Julia was now showing in her son. John would now go and stay with her, her husband and his half-sisters. Julia, too, was a clown, and instead of scolding as Mimi did, she laughed at John's pranks.

Then, in 1956, while John was in the fourth form (4C to be precise, the class for grammar school failures), something happened which at last gave some kind of direction to all the energy he was displaying in rebellious behaviour. Another boy in 4C can take the credit. 'His name was Don Beatty,' said John, 'and his mother was always buying him records and things. One day he showed me a copy of the *New Musical Express* record charts and pointed to something called "Heartbreak Hotel" by Elvis. He said it was great, but I thought it sounded a bit phoney. I'd never heard it. We never listened to pop music in our house. Then one night I heard it on Radio Luxembourg. That was it. Nothing really affected me until Elvis.'

From the distance of twenty-five years it is hard to remember just how startling the effect of Elvis Presley was upon young people everywhere during that spring and summer of 1956, or how cowed by America were the children of those times. That John Lennon would spend the last quarter of his life living in America is not altogether surprising. Britain, particularly working-class Britain, in the late forties and fifties was in many respects a cultural colony of the United States. During the Second World War one and a half million American servicemen had been massed in Britain, and around them sprang up vast airbases like that at Burtonwood just outside Liverpool. 'Have you got any gum, chum,' children would shout to the long convoys of trucks carrying GIs through the English streets. America offered wealth, excitement and abundance. In a port like Liverpool that belief was heightened as the ships trekked to and from New York, dispersing American culture with the incoming soldiers. Even after the war the American link stayed. The base at Burtonwood remained and off-duty American airmen were a common sight. At the Pier Head, where John had been taken by his Uncle George, children would look out down the Mersey and know that the next stop was America.

In the early fifties most of the little good popular music that existed (Johnnie Ray, Frankie Laine and Guy Mitchell) was American, while the films which were popular with young people (cowboy, action, and adventure movies) were invariably American. To grow up in a working-class environment in England in the forties and fifties was, in many respects, to live a second-hand American life. Everything that was new was American. And then came Elvis.

For the rest of his life John Lennon would insist that he was basically a rocker. He loved rock and roll with a passion. It was his music. It was his time. For John, nobody in rock and roll ever improved on Jerry Lee Lewis's record 'Whole Lotta Shakin''.

In later years John Lennon seemed to represent and almost to shape the culture of the times. But he was himself, as he would have been the first to admit, a creature of his own times. That he was fifteen when Elvis hit him was one of those accidents of fate. Had he been aged ten or twenty he would undoubtedly have turned into a different man – perhaps an eccentric art teacher, or possibly another Liverpool comedian, or perhaps simply an entertaining, likeable ship's steward with ideas above his station. But at fifteen his life was shaped. 'My first Pied Piper was rock and roll,' he liked to say. 'When I heard it I dropped everything.'

Auntie Mimi was, however, not quite so impressed. As a child he had not shown any great interest in music. She had considered piano lessons, but he would have been too undisciplined to practise, and the only instrument he had mastered had been a mouth organ which his Uncle George had bought for him. Now he wanted a guitar. Between them, Lonnie Donegan and Elvis Presley had democratized popular music. Earlier in the year Lonnie Donegan had had a big hit in the skiffle style with 'Rock Island Line', an Appalachian country song, and all over Britain boys were banding together to form groups on guitar, washboard and home-made, stand-up string bass. Everyone really wanted to be Elvis, but the first Presley records to be released in Britain had him singing with the aid of an echo chamber and electric guitars. It was obviously impossible to copy his sound when you were fifteen and playing in someone's front room. But anyone could be in a skiffle group . . . or at least that was the way it seemed to the young hopefuls of 1956.

Against her better judgment, Mimi bought John his first guitar. (It was once thought that Julia was the benevolent encourager of young talent. It is certainly a more romantic notion, and one which would have appealed to John, but it was almost certainly a reluctant Mimi who actually nurtured the growing obsession with a cheap Spanish guitar.) Ten years earlier, Elvis Presley's father had admonished his son with the advice that 'he never knew a guitar player who ever made a dime'; now Mimi was to take up the refrain: 'The guitar's all right, John. But you'll never make a living with it.'

Even if Julia did not actually buy that first guitar it was certainly she who taught John the first chords he was to play. As a girl she had sung and played banjo, and it was banjo chords that she taught John. By now he was sixteen and in his final year at Quarry Bank. All ambitious boys were already swotting for their GCEs which took place the following June, but John Lennon was busy forming his own group. Naturally enough he called it the

Quarrymen, and it comprised any of the boys in his school gang who showed any musical ability and several who didn't. The personnel changed by the week as John rowed first with one and then another. 'If you'd been in my class at school I'd have had *you* in the Quarrymen,' he later told me. 'I would have *made* you join to rebel against your mother.' Anyone who liked rock and roll could join. John, of course, was the leader of the group. He didn't know any other way. From childhood he had always assumed an attitude of natural superiority.

Throughout that final year at school John wandered deeper into the world of rock music. Again it was an American culture which was being imposed from outside. It was a full year before Cliff Richard came up with 'Move It', a full year before any British act would make a proper rock and roll record, and it was nearly a year before John would meet Paul McCartney. For a year, while the embryonic Quarrymen larked about with John practising in the porch of his home, the craze grew, and the newspapers began to devote more and more space to this new phenomenon, linking it with violence and the screen rebel heroes of James Dean (who was dead before Elvis even had a hit record) and Marlon Brando. At night, instead of doing his homework, John would tune the family radio in to the weak signal of AFN Munich so that he could hear the new American records before anyone else, or he would listen to the more accessible Radio Luxembourg. (The BBC took a dim view of rock and roll music and devoted as little time to it as was humanly possible in those days.) By this time John was beginning to dress in the Teddy Boy style of the times, tight trousers and greasy hair swept back and up into a pompadour on top of his head. Poor Mimi suffered it all, but never in silence.

John was always funny in his reflections on those adolescent days. When the exploitation film *Rock Around the Clock* was released in Britain there was much written in the papers about how it caused violence among young people. Naturally enough John had to see this for himself. Later he expressed his disappointment at the sedateness of the evening with mock mortification. 'I was most surprised. Nobody was screaming and nobody was dancing. I mean I'd read that everybody danced in the aisles. It must have all been done before I got there. I was all set to tear up the seats, too, but nobody joined in.' Writer Maureen Cleave remembers John telling her of one of the terrible moments of decision which faced him during those first few months of rock and roll. He told her: 'This boy at school had been to Holland. He said he'd got this record at home by somebody who was better than Elvis. Elvis was bigger than religion in my life. We used to go to this boy's house and listen to Elvis on 78s; we'd buy five Senior Service loose in this shop, and some chips and we'd go along. The new record was "Long Tall Sally". When I heard it, it was so great I couldn't speak. You know how you are torn. I didn't want to leave Elvis. We all looked at each other, but I didn't want to say anything against Elvis, not even in my mind. How could they be happening in my life, *both* of them. And then someone said: "It's a nigger singing." I didn't know Negroes sang. So Elvis was white and Little Richard was black. "Thank you, God," I said. There was a difference between them. But I thought about it for days at school, of the labels on the records. One was yellow (Little Richard) and one was blue, and I thought of the yellow against the blue.'

These were the stories John would tell for the rest of his life with happy affection and self-deprecating earnestness. With such cosmic thoughts inside his head it was hardly surprising that his final year at school was to end in failure in all eight GCE ordinary levels, including art and English language. When John got a passion about something, anything, he didn't mess about. When he didn't . . . he did.

All the time his macho view of himself was growing. He was never in any street fights or a delinquent, but he liked to dress and act tough. In many ways his life at that age was a pretence. He told Jonathan Cott of *Rolling Stone*: 'I spent the whole of my childhood with my shoulders up around the top of my head and my glasses off, because glasses were sissy, walking in complete fear but with the toughest looking little face you've ever seen. I'd get into trouble just because of the way I looked: I wanted to be this tough James Dean.'

Throughout the early part of 1957 the Quarrymen played in their homes, at street parties and weddings, usually for nothing or at the most a few shillings. When the Crickets' record, 'That'll Be the Day', was released Julia taught John more chords, and that became the first song he could play properly. 'Ain't That a Shame' was another. By now rock and roll had a galaxy of stars like Fats Domino, Ricky Nelson, the Everly Brothers, Gene Vincent and Eddie Cochran. They were all gods to John.

On 6 July 1957, not long after completing his 'O' levels, John took the Quarrymen to the local Woolton Parish Church's annual garden party where they were to play. Loyal friend Ivan Vaughan had chosen this occasion as the day John should meet a younger boy from the Liverpool Institute, a fourteen-year-old who was also obsessed with Elvis and Buddy Holly. So John Lennon, his breath smelling strongly of beer, met Paul McCartney, who had gone on his bicycle from nearby Allerton. The Quarrymen did a few variations of songs like 'Maggie May', the Del Vikings' 'Come Go with Me' and Gene Vincent's 'Be-Bop-a-Lula', the words of which John improvised because he didn't know all the lyrics. Paul thought they were quite good.

Afterwards in the Church Hall Paul showed them what he could do, including his version of the Eddie Cochran hit, 'Twenty Flight Rock'. John had to be impressed because technically Paul was a more competent guitarist than he was. He leaned over Paul's shoulder all the time to learn the chords to 'Twenty Flight Rock'. He was also impressed by the fact that Paul had begun writing his own songs, and also because he could sing. He did not, however, decide to take him into the Quarrymen immediately. He wanted him in because he was so obviously good, far better than any of the classmates who had made up the group so far. But there were two problems: John had to be the leader in everything he did, and whoever heard of a group with two lead singers? At the same time John's commercial brain was telling him that Paul, who 'looked like Elvis', had a lot of talent. A week later Paul bumped into Pete Shotton. Pete had a message. Did Paul want to join the group? He did.

The inclusion of Paul into the Quarrymen was more than simply the addition of a new guitarist. It was the spur John needed to take up writing seriously. Much has been written of how the comradeship of the Lennon and McCartney partnership soured in later years and turned into rivalry. But, in fact, although they were friends, they were always rivals, too. 'I learned a lot from Paul,' said John. 'He knew more about how to play than I did and he showed me a lot of chords. I'd been playing the guitar like a banjo so I had to learn it again. I started to write after Paul did a song he'd written.' Nothing breeds ambition like competition. Among the earliest songs John wrote were 'One After 909', which over a decade later Paul was to sing on the last Beatles album *Let It Be*, and 'Hello Little Girl', a song the Beatles eventually gave away to another Liverpool group, the Fourmost.

Paul's background was decidedly more working class than that of John. His father, Jim McCartney, worked in the cotton industry and his income was always very low. But he was one of nature's kind and true gentlemen, the sort of man who would never visit the house of friends, or later the friends of his sons, without finding half a crown to give to each of the children for a treat. He was old-fashioned, philosophical, and, like all parents of the fifties, he wanted his sons to have the opportunities he had missed. He was thirty-nine when he married, and when he was widowed at the age of fifty-three he had a considerable struggle to bring up his two sons without a mother, who, as a nursing sister, had actually earned more than he had. But the McCartneys were a closely knit clan and there was always help from Jim's two sisters, Auntie Jinny and Auntie Millie. There is no doubt that the ever conservative Jim McCartney was worried when his elder son seemed to be turning into a Teddy Boy and mixing with John Lennon, but he always encouraged him with his music. And later, when Paul did very badly in his GCE 'O' levels (he passed only one at the first attempt), Jim did not insist upon Paul immediately finding a job as other parents might have done. Instead he found the funds to allow Paul to stay at school, take his failed subjects again, and go on into the sixth form, from where he hoped he would progress to a teacher's training college – a truly respectable goal for Jim McCartney's generation.

Despite the age difference (when you are fourteen years old, sixteen seems positively grown up) John and Paul became close friends and would meet at Paul's home in Forthlin Road. Paul's mother had died of cancer about a year earlier and because Paul and his younger brother Michael had largely to fend for themselves until their father came home from work the front room of their home became something of a rehearsal room for the new partnership of Lennon and McCartney. Paul had had a much more musical background than John, his father having once played in a traditional jazz band himself, and he was therefore steeped in all kinds of popular music – a facet of his character which was eventually to turn Beatle albums into musical variety shows and aggravate the life out of his co-writer.

It is difficult to imagine two more different temperaments than John Lennon and Paul McCartney. Paul was, and still is, always the hard-working, eager-beaver, charming little diplomat – the perfect PR who hid his massive ego behind a fetching smile. John was reckless, given to wild passions and obsessions, academically lazy, witty, acerbic, and straight-talking. While Paul had a very strong streak of conservatism running through him, John, despite Mimi's coaching in the social graces, was totally anti-establishment. They were as different as boys can be, and yet united by the common bond of music. Gradually the Quarrymen were taking shape, and one by one John's childhood friends Pete and Ivan were being replaced by more ambitious musicians. And in 1958 Paul introduced another boy from the Liverpool Institute called George Harrison, who was even younger than Paul.

In John's eyes George was little more than a baby, three years younger and 'always tagging along'. In fact he was often embarrassed to be seen with George so great was the age gap. Also, at that time, George had no illusions of himself as a misunderstood intellectual. He was not academically good and when he left the Institute he took a job as a trainee electrician. In Mimi's eyes he was a really rough-looking little Ted, with a very working-class accent (his father was a bus driver) – an observation which probably worked in his favour so far as John was concerned. What worked mostly in his favour, however, was his ability on the guitar. It was the one thing he could do well, and he practised hard and long at it, with the full co-operation of his parents. Years later Brian Epstein would say that George was the most musical of the Beatles. That was probably partly to encourage him, but also because by years of practice George had a far better grasp of the complexities required to be a good virtuoso musician. When he joined the Quarrymen it was right that he played lead guitar, despite his youth. George also had something else going for him. He was nice, a naturally far more likeable person than Paul who could be a bully, and John who, although usually funny, was often cuttingly cruel. It may have been a drag for John to have this kid tagging on to him, but at least George was a nice kid, and loyal to a fault. And unlike Paul, who always had a pretty grand idea of himself, George hero-worshipped John.

By this time John had enrolled at Liverpool Art College, with the help of a particularly understanding and forgiving headmaster at Quarry Bank. Normally students who don't get a single pass in their GCEs do not get a chance to go to college. John was lucky. If he was ever grateful, and there was never any suggestion that he was, he did not show it by working hard. He could not understand why no one realized that he was a great artist, and soon found himself stuck in the lettering class, which was as likely a place to find him as an insurance office. To do lettering you had to be neat and, if possible, totally non-creative. John was never neat, and totally creative. But at last he had been able to get rid of his grammar school blazer and tie and dress in a style more suited to his macho image of himself.

Recollections of John at this time in his life are varied. Michael McGear (Paul McCartney's younger brother who also went to the Liverpool Institute and who would see John hanging around outside the Art College and at their home in Forthlin Road) also hero-worshipped him. 'There were never any compromises with John,' he says. 'He was a very simple, complex man, if you know what I mean. He'd never use two words where one would do. He was like a young, hungry animal.'

Other contemporaries were less flattering. By the time he had reached Art College John had developed a particularly cruel and perverse sense of humour. He was always surrounded by a crowd of fawning followers, but his behaviour could be brutal and unkind, particularly towards his early girlfriends. 'I used to be cruel to my woman, I beat her, and kept her apart from the things that she loved,' he and Paul would write for the song 'Getting Better' on the *Sergeant Pepper* album, and he was later to admit that it summarized his early attitude towards girls very well. Art College classmates remember being in awe of John, with his Teddy Boy clothes (while they were all wearing the baggy sweaters of the art student world), his habit of borrowing money which was never returned, his sick cartoons and his cruel sense of humour in which he would imitate hunchbacks or other deformed people. He was not handsome in the style of the day ('Paul was the one with girl appeal,' he would later admit), but his wit and individuality compensated more than adequately. It's fair to say he was a star before he was a star.

Although John's efforts at the Art College were always negligible, there were wider benefits to be gained. Most obviously was the fact that the Art College was situated in the centre of the Bohemian Liverpool 8 area, near to the university and right next door to the Liverpool Institute, where Paul and George were still at school. So although John despised George for tagging on behind him in lunch hours and after college, the proximity of all three meant even more opportunities for rehearsals and discussions. The Art College also introduced John to people with a wider range of backgrounds and lifestyles than he had ever been used to in suburban Woolton, people with more free and independent ways. In those days Liverpool 8 was a sort of Merseyside Left Bank. Originally the area had been a development of grand Georgian terraces built for the merchant class which turned Liverpool into a major port in the early nineteenth century, but by 1958 the houses had been largely converted into cheap flats and bedsitters, where students, actors, artists, prostitutes and priests would gather in the two most famous pubs, the Crack and the Philharmonic. If Liverpool had any kind of cultural melting pot it was to be found in Liverpool 8, in the pubs, the Jacaranda coffee bar and the Blue Angel club.

Throughout his first year at Art College John kept in close touch with his mother Julia, and the man with whom she lived, who John called Twitchy. Because she was so zany, and because she had been absent so much when he had been a little boy, John regarded her more as a sister than a mother. She was a kindred spirit in his lunacy. Then, towards the end of his first year at college, she was run over by an off-duty policeman just a couple of hundred yards from where Auntie Mimi lived. John was seventeen and very bitter. He felt as though he had been deserted twice in his life. Despite his abiding affection for Auntie Mimi the loss of his real mother seemed to isolate him even further from his contemporaries. And whenever John felt isolated he would always act aggressively. His behaviour towards girls worsened. Mentally he seemed to peel away the skin of childhood forever at that point. Throughout the rest of his life he would continue to peel away one lifestyle after another only to resurface as a different person. He rarely looked backwards, but twelve years later he would write and record a simple, plaintive nursery rhyme: 'My Mummy's dead, It's hard to explain so much pain, I could never show it, My Mummy's dead.'

Dig a Moondog,
Roll a Stoney

Although he continued to see Paul and George regularly during this period there were now two new influences upon John. One was a reputedly brilliant art student called Stuart Sutcliffe, a boy of the same age who had a flat in Gambia Terrace, near the Art College. In many respects John's initial affection and loyalty towards Stu was not dissimilar from the way he was later to regard Yoko Ono. He respected his talent, and his air of freedom. Stu lived the life of the sensitive, vulnerable artist in a garret, and, although John would always profess profound dislike of the bullshit surrounding art, he was attracted to this romantic image. So attracted, in fact, that he even suggested that Stu should invest sixty pounds he had won in an art competition in a bass guitar and join the Quarrymen (who admittedly desperately needed a bass guitar), although he had no real ability as a musician and was never to make a success of it. Twelve years later when he insisted that Yoko Ono join him on stage and record his army of fans were confused. But John was only following his own precedent. To him an artist was an artist, whether he held a paint brush or a guitar. He always found it hard to believe that the same person could not do both, and with Stu and Yoko he refused to accept even the testimony of his own ears.

The other newcomer into his life was a rather secretarial twin-set-and-pearls girl from the Wirral called Cynthia Powell. To people in Liverpool anyone living across the Mersey in the Wirral was posh, and Cynthia Powell was no exception, although her terraced cottage background was as humble as anyone else's. To Cynthia John was a very rough diamond indeed, who held court the whole time, was frighteningly aggressive, but always very funny. In her autobiography *A Twist of Lennon* she recalls how John first enquired about her availability. Terrified of the prospects of this angry young man she lied: 'I'm awfully sorry, I'm engaged to this fellow in Hoylake.' Cut to the quick, John fired back, 'I didn't ask you to marry me, did I?' Four years later he did just that.

The start of their relationship was intense and emotional. He was eighteen and she was nineteen. Later Cynthia would write: 'John's jealousy and possessiveness were at times unbearable, and I found myself a quaking, nervous wreck on many an occasion.' His moods were totally unpredictable: his temper and language were savage.

In 1959 John moved out of Mimi's home in Woolton and into Stuart's flat in Gambia Terrace, a place of considerable squalor, little furniture and masses of half-empty tubes of paint, half-finished canvases and half-eaten sandwiches. It was an admirable arrangement. Stu encouraged John in his art, while John helped Stu learn the bass guitar. The Quarrymen were still struggling along. Paul and John were still writing together, all the lyrics going into one of Paul's exercise books under their dual authorship, an arrangement they had reached on a handshake and which was eventually to lead to not a little misunderstanding. Why they should always have stuck both their names on to all their songs, when often one partner was so much more responsible than the other, is still unclear. It may have been a manifestation of the camaraderie of youth, or simply because nearly all the songwriters of those days seemed to work in pairs . . . Doc Pomus and Mort Schuman, Leiber and Stoller, Goffin and King. Even when Paul or John came up with a song completely by himself, as was later the case with Paul's 'Yesterday', they still shared the credits and the financial rewards. It was a touching, perhaps the only touching, aspect of their relationship.

The arrangement in Gambia Terrace also suited Cynthia, since it meant that she and John had somewhere convenient to sleep together. In those days there was never any question that she should leave her mother's home in Hoylake and move in with John. Even among art students it was rare to find a couple setting up home together in 1959 before they were married.

The financial rewards for being in the Quarrymen at that time were not exactly bewitching and they rarely earned more than a couple of pounds a night. The basic trouble with the group was that they had three guitarists, no proper bass player since Stu was so hopeless, no drummer and no proper equipment. George Harrison could undoubtedly have made a better career for himself by joining one of the more professional groups of the time who were aware of his prowess, but he didn't. Of course, they were all still very young, just two schoolboys and two college students. Still, they did get gigs, places like the Finch Lane bus depot party (George's father worked there) and eventually they even got selected to appear in one of the heats to a Carroll Levis *TV Discoveries* show which took place in Manchester. It was at this point that the name Quarrymen finally disappeared, to be replaced for a short time by Johnny and the Moondogs. The change of name did not help their fortune. The Moondogs did not go on to become one of Mr Levis's discoveries. They went back to Liverpool and changed their name again. This time they became the Beatles, after a short aberration when they took the rather grandiose showbiz title of the Silver Beatles.

The first regular gigs that the Beatles were to get came ironically through the one Beatle who could not play, Stu. Because of his friendship with a local Liverpool hustler Allan Williams the four began to appear in the basement of Williams's coffee bar known as the Jacaranda, a meeting place for itinerant scrubbers, students and all kinds of rag, tag and bobtail people from Liverpool 8. Because the Beatles were still at college or school most of the gigs were in the lunch hour, and the line-up was still very basic. They were still without a drummer and Stu's bass playing had hardly improved. But in their black Marks and Spencer polo-neck sweaters, black jeans and white gym shoes they at least were beginning to look like a group, and what they lacked in professionalism they made up for in energy and enthusiasm, playing in front of borrowed amplifiers and speakers, and trying to cover up for Stu on bass. Other groups also played at the Jacaranda, minor local stars like Rory Storm and the Hurricanes, who had a drummer called Ringo Starr, and Cass and the Casanovas.

By 1959 a great deal had happened in the rock and roll world which was to affect the Beatles. Buddy Holly and Eddie Cochran were both dead, Chuck Berry was in jail. Elvis was being musically emasculated in the US Army, and the first generation of British rock and rollers were enjoying their first flush of success. Like all true connoisseurs of rock music the Beatles found their more successful contemporaries cringingly embarrassing: after one good record with 'Move It', Cliff Richard was becoming increasingly wet, Tommy Steele had always been a hyped-up joke for the media (a good family entertainer, but never a rocker), Wee Willie Harris was an even worse joke, and, while Marty Wilde and Billy Fury undoubtedly had talent, it was a derivative talent, seemingly based on whatever happened to be doing well in the American charts. Even American rock and roll was going soft, it seemed, with newcomers like Bobby Vee, Fabian, Bobbie Vinton and Frankie Avalon singing teenage laments about high school proms and graduation rings. This was not the music that had first attracted John Lennon and Paul McCartney. When Elvis had started it had all been straight from the gut lust, a sound produced apparently by mainlining virility and passion. He had taken black rhythm and blues music and bleached it into a steaming poor white rock driven along by jangling guitars and an eruption of nervous energy. Chuck Berry and Buddy Holly had adopted that sound, and given it a new literacy, observations on the American way of auto-life in the case of Chuck Berry, and whimsical, clever, sad little love songs from Buddy Holly. But most of the newer sounds were simply pale shadows of that music, augmented and softened now with orchestral backing or pizzicato strings. The Beatles hated it.

They may not exactly have hated Billy Fury, but then neither did they love him either. He was from Liverpool himself but had become a very big star in the moody Elvis mould while they had been beavering along at school. But it was Billy Fury who first suggested that they be given a decent break. The incident occurred when impresario Larry Parnes, Fury's manager, was looking for a group to accompany Fury on a tour. At Allan Williams's suggestion Parnes and Fury came to Liverpool to audition some of the local groups. The audition took place in Williams's new club The Blue Angel.

As always the Beatles were short of a drummer for the audition (a drum kit was very expensive, so drummers were always in short supply) but they borrowed somebody and played along with the other groups for Parnes and Fury. Fury wanted the Beatles, but Parnes was worried about the bass player. Stu had played with his back to Parnes during the whole audition because he actually couldn't play, but Parnes hadn't been fooled. He asked if the group would play again without the boy on bass. 'No,' said John, with a loyalty which was not to turn into a lifelong habit. Either Parnes wanted them with Stu, or not at all.

Parnes chose to live without them on that occasion, but a few months later he booked them for a tour with one of his less prestigious protégés, a youth named Johnny Gentle. (All of Parnes's boys had names like Wilde, Fury or Gentle.) Again they found themselves a fill-in drummer and set off on their first tour. It was not a success. Although they took Stu (who was not being paid) along with them, they used to pull the lead out of his amp so bad was his playing, and although he was John's friend this did not prevent him becoming the butt of a great deal of the more vicious Lennon humour. It is worth remembering that not everyone liked John Lennon. To many people he was a mean, vicious and cruel man who made fun of authority and scoffed at weakness. He could behave like a complete bastard, and frequently did – as he was openly to admit many years later.

In the summer of 1960 Paul left school with one 'A' level (in Art) and to no one's surprise John was kicked out of Art College. Allan Williams, their friend and de facto manager, got them a booking in Hamburg. From now on they were no longer part-time students and part-time musicians: all three, plus Stu, and a new drummer they had picked up called Pete Best, were to become full-time musicians. The Beatle sound was about to be conceived.

When the Beatles finally emerged to national and then international prominence there was genuine surprise in the pop world at their technical abilities and apparently limitless repertoire. How could four unknown men play so well, write so originally, sing in such close harmony and be so totally self-confident and professional? The answer lay basically in Hamburg. Unlike most British rock stars, the Beatles had years of playing and writing together before they became famous. They had masses of opportunities to make their mistakes and learn from them before being catapulted into the public gaze. Had they won the Carroll Levis *Discoveries* show they would most probably have withered and died before very long; had Larry Parnes recognized the budding talent they would have been robbed of their opportunities to experiment, and found themselves with some butch name and mohair suits long before they were ready for success. As it was, the world took an awful long time to recognize the Beatles, and when it did they had paid more than their dues. They were good and they knew it.

In Liverpool they had already built up a small following before going to Hamburg, but it was in the long tortuous hours of playing on stage in the small sleazy India Club in Hamburg that they were to begin to graduate from being just a good rock and roll band, to being the best group in the world. Billy Fury, Marty Wilde, Cliff Richard and Adam Faith all had it much easier. They got to the top very quickly, without having time to really learn their trade, and it was only Cliff Richard among the dozens of early British rock stars who was to make any lasting impression. Phil Spector used to say that you can't hide talent; but sometimes talent needs hiding while it is being nursed. In Liverpool the longest gig the Beatles had ever played was an hour. In Hamburg they were expected to go out and entertain for as long as eight hours at a stretch. No wonder they got good. They were given the opportunity to fail, to rehearse and improvise before an audience. And when it came to rock and roll they recognized and were grateful for their opportunities.

Domestic arrangements on that first visit to Hamburg were primitive, all five boys sleeping in one room behind a cinema screen. They did everything together. Everything. Apart from the girls, there was drink and there were pep pills. At first they started on Preludin, slimming pills, because they were told that that was the way to stay awake during their marathon playing stints; and then they graduated to whatever else was available, usually purple hearts, which, combined with the alcohol they were consuming, made them even loonier.

Before long they moved to another, larger club called the Kaiserkeller, and more marathon sessions, in which they had to play very loudly to get their drunken unruly audiences to pay any attention at all. None of the Beatles had much knowledge of the German language and John never even bothered to try and learn. They were rough bars, where the waiters carried flick knives, and sailors would get drunk and brawl while the Beatles played deafeningly on. When the Beatles weren't playing, Rory Storm and the Hurricanes were, driven along by Ringo's steady drumming. Of course there were still arguments in the group, particularly between Paul and Stu. Paul had been John's special friend until Stu had come along. Paul probably resented him. And Stu was still having trouble with his bass guitar.

The Beatles stayed in Hamburg for five months on that first occasion. Of course the local rockers liked them, but they were now taken up by a new force of fans from the local art college including Klaus Voorman and his girlfriend Astrid Kirchherr, the first in the never ending line of self-considered intellectuals who were to become Beatle fans. Klaus was also a musician and was eventually to turn up in England in the mid-sixties to illustrate the cover to the *Revolver* album and play bass with John on several solo albums including *Imagine*. Over the next few months Astrid set about photographing them, moody black and white pictures, encouraging them to wear black leather, and eventually to comb their hair forward.

Then just before Christmas 1960 they ran into trouble. George was deported because at seventeen he was under age, and Paul and Pete Best were thrown into jail after accidentally starting a fire in the room in which they lived.

One by one the Beatles drifted back to Liverpool. The great adventure had ended in failure. They were all broke. Only Stu had done well: he had fallen in love with the enigmatic Astrid. John went home to Mimi and got his customary scolding, and dropped out of sight for a while. He wasn't even sure whether he wanted to continue with the Beatles, he was to say later. John may have been the exhibitionist on stage, he may have talked more than virtually anybody in the world but, even then, he was always prone to states of reclusivity.

The need to work brought him out of it. At first they played a few gigs at Pete Best's mother's club, The Casbah, and then just after Christmas, 1960, they appeared at Litherland Town Hall. It was then that they first realized that something had changed while they had been in Hamburg. Suddenly they had fans. They were unlike anything or anybody else. John would say later that they were the first punks. A few weeks later they began making regular appearances at The Cavern club in the city centre, mainly during the lunch hour since evenings were reserved for trad jazz. Their fans became more numerous. Their fame was spreading like wildfire around Liverpool. They looked and sounded different, and alongside the thin, over-rehearsed rock groups of the day, who usually played variations of the Shadows' sound, their music was positively brutal. Altogether they were to make over 250 appearances at The Cavern.

Later in the year they returned to Hamburg, and this time they even made a record, with John singing 'My Bonnie Lies Over the Ocean' for Bert Kaempfert's company. Later, when it was released in America at the height of Beatlemania, it was a huge success, but John always hated it. It was on this trip that Stu eventually decided that he was never going to be happy as a musician, and left to join the local art college. Paul finally took over the bass guitar. For a year John and Stu wrote to each other, long letters of affection. Then in April 1962 Stu died of a brain haemorrhage. He had never been cut out to be a musician, but he was certainly an artist of some promise, and certainly more intellectually able than the other Beatles. Although John had teased him mercilessly about his bad playing, and had not been particularly distressed when he voluntarily left the group, Stu's death hit John badly. Stu had been an intellectual soul-mate.

Altogether the Beatles made five trips to Hamburg and each time they made a bigger impression. Each time Cynthia stayed at home – the steady girlfriend, while John wallowed in excesses of sex, pills and drink. Cynthia was the archetypal rock and roll widow. Whenever they were in Liverpool the Beatles appeared at The Cavern or local dance halls. Very, very slowly their earnings were increasing, but still no record company had come along to whisk them away to fame and fortune. Part of the trouble was that they no longer had a manager, due to a disagreement with Allan Williams, and there was no one to realize their abilities. All the record companies were based in London and in those days Liverpool was a very long way away.

Then in October 1961 Brian Epstein, then twenty-seven, and the manager of one of his family's Liverpool music shops, was asked for a copy of 'My Bonnie'. Later in the day he was asked again. He had never heard of the Beatles, but an acquaintance had. He was told he could see them at The Cavern where they were performing. The club was dank with sweat, excitement and poor draining, the music was deafening, and the four boys on stage looked extremely rough. But they had presence, they generated excitement, and they were funny. After the show he asked if he could be their manager. They agreed. They had nothing to lose. To them Epstein was a man of some sophistication.

Much has been made of Epstein's homosexuality in deciding to manage the Beatles. But probably not even he ever really knew what were his true motives. He had been to RADA, without much success, and clearly was attracted by the bright lights. Perhaps he really did think the Beatles would be 'bigger than Elvis', as he claimed a year later. But that was more probably hindsight. In all likelihood he was simply a fairly well-off young man, attracted to the four unkempt individuals who had no respect for anything, least of all him, and who, unlike him, had not had so much of their personalities repressed by guilt, family, religion and school. They were originals, led by the most original of all – John Lennon, a totally reckless, lunatic character, who was witty, and always fun to be with. 'Brian loved John because he made him laugh so much,' a mutual friend would say. Brian was actually completely infatuated with John.

Throughout 1961 and the first half of 1962 the Beatles bided their time, sometimes playing as many as three gigs a day. But they were still no more than local heroes. A new Merseyside music paper called *Mersey Beat*, edited by a local boy called Bill Harry, voted them the best group, largely because the Beatles bought up hundreds of copies of the paper and therefore rigged the votes. But it was much harder to get any straight press coverage. The *Liverpool Echo* would have been the most obvious place for them to have been written about, but when a reporter called Vincent Kelly went along to The Cavern to interview them he was put off by some wisecrack by John and never bothered to write his story. They tried again with the *Echo* diarist, named, coincidentally, George Harrison, a man who was reputed to know everyone on Merseyside. He didn't want to know anyone called the Beatles, namesake or not, and it was eventually left to a mild, gentle,

1. John, aged four.

2. A rare picture of John in a tuxedo, dancing with George Harrison's mother after the première of *A Hard Day's Night* in 1964.

3. John was twenty-four before he passed his driving test. He rarely drove himself, anyway.

4. John with his first wife, Cynthia, at the première of *Help!* The Beatles said later they felt like extras in the film.

5. *Above:* for the first time, during a guest appearance in the BBC programme *Not Only, But Also* in 1966, John allows himself to be seen with his little granny glasses. *Below:* by the time of the filming of *Magical Mystery Tour* in September 1967 the eccentric artist had taken over from the semi-glamorous millionaire pop star of the mid-sixties.

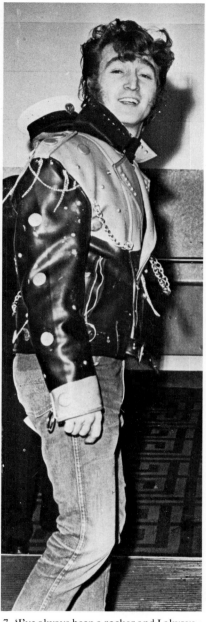

6. *Above:* a rare picture of John with his son Julian (during the filming of *Magical Mystery Tour*). *Below:* in 1967 this psychedelically painted Rolls caused consternation among the Lennons' Weybridge neighbours who thought it an eye-sore. Rolls-Royce were not amused either.

7. 'I've always been a rocker and I always · will be,' John would often say. At a party to celebrate *Magical Mystery Tour* he showed what he meant.

8. The opening of the Apple boutique in Baker Street. Nine months later all the goods were given away free.

9. Appearing in Dick Lester's anti-war film, *How I Won the War*, in 1966. 'I hate war. If there is another war I won't fight and I'll tell all the youngsters not to fight either,' said John.

10. John at his first avant-garde art exhibition at the Robert Frazer Gallery in the summer of 1968. He was stung by the reviewers' negative response, but he carried on.

11. The Lennon Bed-ins became a regular feature of their life in the late sixties. Here (1969) they are leaving for the Bahamas along with Yoko's six-year-old daughter, Kyoko, by a previous marriage.

12. There was something heroic about the way John protected Yoko from a jeering public after they were arrested on a drugs charge in October 1969. He looked frail and frightened.

13. In 1968 John and Yoko became inseparable. Here they attend the first night of a play based on his book *In His Own Write* at the Old Vic.

14. John was a chameleon figure. He seemed to change disguise every few months. When he and Yoko arrived back from Denmark in 1969 they had had their hair shorn off. They later donated it to Michael X's notorious Black House venture.

15. Always John had one protective arm around Yoko. (May 1971)

16. The Lennons as they move into their beautiful Georgian home, Tittenhurst Park, in 1971. Question: who is the third 'Virgin' in the picture on the left?

17. John with Yoko's former secretary, May Pang, during his eighteen-month 'lost weekend' in which the Lennons split up. (1974)

18. Between 1975, when the US Immigration Court granted him a permanent resident visa, and 1980, John lived as a recluse in his New York home.

19. One of the few pictures that show John with his second son, Sean, born in 1975. They enter the Dakota apartment building where they lived and where John died.

middle-aged reporter, Bill Rogers, standing in on the diary one week when Harrison was on holiday, to give them their first mass-circulation publicity.

Meanwhile, Brian Epstein was setting about getting them a recording contract. The most famous story is of how a man at Decca called Dick Rowe turned the Beatles down with a suggestion that groups of guitarists were on the way out. The fact is, as the Beatles would point out later, they did a bad audition for him that day. It was the first time they had played in London and they were terrified. But for twenty years Dick Rowe has been the butt of every possible music business joke.

'Dick Rowe must be kicking himself now,' Paul said a year later.

'I hope he kicks himself to death,' said John.

There were other rejections, too. Pye didn't want to know, and Epstein had no better success with EMI's two most popular labels, Columbia and His Master's Voice. But while the London record companies refused to listen the Beatles continued to play, and John and Paul continued to write, John also now showing his more literary side by contributing a gobbledegook column to the *Mersey Beat*.

Finally Epstein got an interview with producer George Martin at Parlophone, the least fashionable of all the EMI labels. Martin had a reputation for making comedy records with Bernard Cribbins and Peter Sellers. Martin liked the acetates that Epstein played and decided to take a risk on the Beatles – at a penny a record it wasn't a very big risk. But before that could happen there were to be two changes. Although Pete Best had now been playing regularly with them for two years the other three wanted to get rid of him. Ringo Starr had left Rory Storm. He was available. For years Pete Best has, understandably, bemoaned the fact that the Beatles dropped him on the eve of fame, but many who saw the Beatles in those days have observed that Best simply seemed out of touch with the other three. Being cowards, they left it to Epstein to break the news to the unsuspecting Best.

The other change involved John personally. After going out with John for four and a half years whenever he was in Liverpool, Cynthia became pregnant. For John there was only one answer to that. They would get married. Despite all his rebelliousness he remained deeply conservative at heart. In Liverpool in those days if a boy 'got a girl into trouble' he married her. Many years later John would tell interviewers that he never loved Cynthia and only married her because she was pregnant. But his memory about that could be very selective. Throughout all the long trips to Hamburg he had continued to send masses of erotic love letters. Had he wanted to disengage himself from the relationship he had more than ample opportunity. But he never did. Cynthia was always there when he got back home, ready with the instant security blanket, and many of the Lennon and McCartney songs of the period concern a boy-girl relationship in which the two are separated ('P.S. I Love You', 'I'll Be Back', 'It Won't Be Long', 'When I Get Home'). Cynthia provided a bedrock of sympathy and understanding for John during their early years together. Although he would have denied it, there was something comforting and secure about the slightly bourgeois life which she seemed to offer, as comforting as Mimi's semi-detached home in Woolton to which he would always retreat whenever things were not going well. He loved his creature comforts, and he had a great need for the mothering kind of affection which Cynthia could provide.

They were married on 23 August 1962, five days after Ringo had joined the group, and one day after they had been filmed playing live at The Cavern by Granada Television. If the *Liverpool Echo* was slow to grasp what was happening two hundred yards down the street from their offices, Granada in Manchester were not. In the section of film which was shown, and which has been shown many thousands of times around the world since, the Beatles sang 'Some Other Guy', another of the rhythm and blues songs which they now preferred to the white rock and roll coming from America.

John's marriage was kept a complete secret. Ringo was not even invited to or told about the event. Mimi did not attend. She was reportedly disgusted. Brian Epstein was best man and the reception was at Reece's Café. For once in their lives the three Beatles present wore suits.

For their first record, producer George Martin chose 'Love Me Do' and 'P.S. I Love You' from a selection of songs which also included 'Hello Little Girl' and 'Ask Me Why'. Even before the record was released, virtually every young person on Merseyside who had any awareness was Beatle-obsessed. Their fame had spread way beyond The Cavern now and was attracting fans from the most unlikely of places, even hick, one-juke-box towns like Ormskirk, and to his eternal embarrassment this writer refused all offers to discover the glory of the Beatles. Some people would be very slow to admit that British groups could make good rock and roll.

Throughout the rest of 1962 they worked continuously. Cynthia moved in with Mimi (since her mother was now working in Canada and Mimi had recovered from the shock) and the Beatle legend began to spread its roots. 'Love Me Do' eventually only reached seventeenth position on the *New Musical Express* charts, but it laid the groundwork. The massive EMI organization had not been particularly impressed with the record, but word of mouth on the Beatles was immense. In December they played their last dates in Hamburg.

The pop music charts were as soft and wishy-washy then as they had ever been. Top of the charts was Cliff Richard with 'Bachelor Boy', next came the Shadows with 'Dance On'. Poor old Elvis was busy making asinine beach-boy movies. The field was wide open for something new. The old names were stale: their sounds were dull, their personalities polished and remote. The end of 1962 saw the collapse of the old show-business style into which Cliff and even Elvis had tried to mould themselves. Their ambition had been to become all-round entertainers, family stars. The last thing in the world that John Lennon would ever desire was to become an all-rounder. He just wanted to be rich and famous, but rich and famous on his terms.

The Beatles act by 1962 was probably at its peak so far as hard rock and roll was concerned. John said: 'We could play for hours. I know every rock and roll song much better than any of the ones I've written myself. We would do ten- and fifteen-minute versions of early Elvis things like "Baby Let's Play House" and the Carl Perkins version of "Blue Suede Shoes"; and then, of course, there were all those great Chuck Berry things, doing the same verses over and over again. We would just go on and on until our voices hurt from so much singing.' Although they wrote prolifically, it was not their own songs that the fans wanted to hear at first. Like all fans familiar songs were more popular than new ones so the Beatles obliged with 'Dizzy Miss Lizzy', 'Roll Over Beethoven', 'Woolly Bully', the Isley Brothers' 'Twist and Shout', Little Richard's 'Long Tall Sally', the Marvelettes' 'Please Mr Postman', the Miracles' 'You've Really Got a Hold on Me' and their show-stopper, 'Money'. There had always been a tradition in rock and roll that no one could perform a song as well as the original American hit version. The Beatles stood that idea on its head. They were often as good, and sometimes better than the originals.

During the first few months of 1963 the Beatles were to become the biggest act in Britain. A year later America was to fall to them. They were like a conquering army. Wherever they went the walls of resistance tumbled before them. But the victories were not gained without some compromises, serious compromises so far as John was concerned, but ones which he was happy to go along with at the time.

'We began to sell out when we let Brian begin to manage us,' he would say later. 'He put us into uniforms – suits, and we would go on and smile and do twenty-minute acts of our hits. It was a buzz, but all the fun was to go out of performing. People like Mick Jagger say that we were never a great rock and roll band to watch. But he has no idea. He never saw us at our best in Liverpool and

Hamburg. There was no one to touch us then. We were fantastic. By the time we got to London all the rough edges were being knocked off us. I knew what we were doing, and I knew the game. So I let it happen. We were selling out all right, right from the moment we began to get really big.'

II

The World

About Four Lucky Men
Who Made the Grade

The Beatles were not the sixties; and neither were the sixties the Beatles, although that is how the decade and the group will forever be remembered in the public's consciousness. The Beatles set to music an extraordinary era in post-war history, they provided a musical tapestry for the 'never had it so good' years, the boom time in the Western economies, the years when in Britain the class barriers crumbled for a while, before the straitjacket of privilege was reinforced by recession. Although the Beatles were the most evident and lasting of sixties culture, they were only a part of a series of far wider changes.

It has been pointed out earlier that the fifties were the years of the achievers. The sixties were the years when the grammar school successes, the scholarship boys, were rewarded for their efforts. It was an extraordinary time when the pendulum swung away from repression and opened all kinds of doors. On television David Frost and a team of wits produced the wickedly irreverent satire programme *That Was The Week That Was* in which the most popular weekly target was the Prime Minister, Harold Macmillan, a man from another age of genteel, slightly eccentric privilege. In the West End theatre Peter Cook and Dudley Moore teamed with Jonathan Miller and Allan Bennett and staged *Beyond the Fringe*, which was even more wicked in its lampooning of the establishment. For fifteen years Britain had been cowed by the abundance of America. Now it was the turn of the young Britons. So, while the Conservative Macmillan government stumbled bemusedly through the Profumo crisis, when scurrilous rumour had it that high-class call-girls were virtually a perk of Cabinet office, a whole generation mushroomed overnight to mock and make mischief, to irreverently shake the superstructure of the establishment.

John Lennon and the Beatles were, it seemed, almost created to fill the musical void. They fitted the moment to perfection. All his life Lennon had been bucking authority, lampooning the establishment, out of step with authority and being chastised by it. Now suddenly his attitude was not only respectable but the very height of fashion. Everyone was poking fun at the establishment. Satire was having its most successful time since Jonathan Swift. London was full of young people from working-class backgrounds, achievers every one, marauding down from the north, to fill the London stages, art galleries and television and film studios. For a time the dyke had burst and everything seemed possible. For the Beatles the dyke had burst forever. From then on everything was possible.

Their second record, 'Please Please Me', was released at the beginning of January, 1963. Within a month it was the best-selling record in the country. The cautious George Martin had tried to get them to sing another song, 'How Do You Do It?' by another writer for their second release, and they had recorded it together with 'Hello Little Girl', on which John Lennon sang lead. They were both good tracks. But the Beatles thought they could do better and they were never released. 'Please Please Me' was better, although both the other songs were to become hits for other groups managed by the ever growing Epstein empire. The years of gestation in Hamburg and Liverpool were now to reap extraordinary dividends. There was a polished rawness to their music, John's harmonica underscoring George's lead guitar work, Paul and John singing in close harmony, the soaring falsetto notes, while their lyrics had an earthiness which was unequivocal in its raunchiness. ('Please, please me, oh yeah, like I please you' – they weren't exactly singing songs about holding hands under the apple tree, said a wag at the time, adding that if anyone at the BBC had known what heavy petting was they would probably have banned the song.)

Not only did music change with the coming of the Beatles. Fashion changed, too. The brushed-forward hair which Astrid had encouraged in the Hamburg days became the norm for all young men (and is still the fashion for the vast majority of little schoolboys), while Cuban-heeled boots, tab-collared shirts and collarless jackets became *haute couture*. Their influence was felt everywhere. There was a new self-confidence about.

Suddenly the American styles seemed to be so old-fashioned. As the year progressed first one bastion of establishment thinking fell to the Beatles, only to be followed by another. It seemed that every time one turned on the television the Beatles would be there, grinning and playing, John peering down his long nose short-sightedly, always smiling and joking, always mocking.

The press loved the Beatles, and the Beatles loved the press. John always got on well with newspapermen, because he liked to make them laugh. The whole of Britain had seemingly joined his gang. Brian Epstein was as good as his word. He was never to be a good business manager, but he had a rare talent for promotion. The Beatles entourage grew. Music publisher, singer and songwriter Dick James set up Northern Songs with Lennon and McCartney as the two chief writers. ('When I heard Lennon and McCartney I gave up any ideas I might have had about writing songs myself,' said Dick James), and Brian Epstein moved the headquarters of his Nems Agency down to London. For the Beatles themselves it was non-stop work.

They toured Scotland, then they toured England, as second on the bill to Helen Shapiro. It was a nightmare tour for her from which her career was never to recover. She was the established star and had to follow the Beatles on stage. Throughout the whole of her act the fans chanted for the Beatles to return. The same thing happened when they played support to Chris Montez, an American singer. Halfway through that tour they swapped places.

It was humiliating for him, but it was part of the democracy of rock and roll. No one could follow the Beatles.

Everything happened with a bewildering speed. In one day they recorded their complete first album, made up of songs they had been performing in The Cavern, and virtually all done in single takes. Their third single 'From Me to You' was an immediate hit. Lennon and McCartney could now write hits virtually to order, and those they didn't want for themselves they gave away to Brian Epstein's growing stable of Liverpudlian singers. The work and the jokes never stopped.

The Beatles did not want to be all-round entertainers, but Epstein was softening their edges. Children liked them, because they were, as someone said at the time, 'like little furry animals'. What bad publicity there may have been was quickly sat upon by Epstein and the ever-charming Paul. When John knocked Bob Wooller, the Cavern disc jockey, off his feet for drunkenly implying that John might be homosexual, everyone rushed to cover, and Epstein drove the unfortunate disc jockey to hospital. John told Hunter Davies: 'I smashed him up. I battered his bloody ribs for him. I was pissed at the time.' None of the viciousness had left him, nor his macho image of himself. But when asked for a comment by the *Daily Mirror* he said meekly: 'I don't know why I did it. I'm sorry.'

On 8 April Cynthia gave birth to their son Julian in a Liverpool hospital. John was in Liverpool for the birth, but it was kept strictly secret from the press. A few days later he went to Spain on holiday with Epstein. In the early days there was a great deal of speculation about whether or not John ever did have a homosexual affair with Epstein. John always insisted that he did not. In one of his last interviews he told *Playboy* magazine: 'It was almost a love affair, but not quite. It was never consummated. But we did have a pretty intense relationship. And it was my first experience with someone I knew was a homosexual.'

In October 1963 a new word was minted by social chroniclers: it was Beatlemania. In The Cavern the girls had stood and stomped and danced while the Beatles played. But now as the Beatles continually toured the country, playing theatres and cinemas, a wild hysteria besieged them. The fans no longer went to listen to the music. They went to take part in a mass experience, a ritual of youth.

If you wanted to *listen* to the Beatles you bought their records. Their appearances were now completely chaotic. While the heavy Sunday newspapers began to run long sociological articles about the reasons for Beatlemania, the Beatles themselves were being locked in, trapped by the national hysteria. Between October and December 1963 one large national daily paper found a Beatle story to run on its front page every single day.

Brian Epstein was handling their success, if not their money, with a panache which belied his lack of experience. Even while 'She Loves You' was still topping the charts he decided to go for super-kill and release the follow-up 'I Want to Hold Your Hand' before Christmas, just one week before their second album. But before that came the Beatles were even to woo royalty when they appeared in the Royal Command Performance at the London Palladium. Naturally enough they were terrified. One of them had to say something. It was John. Backstage during rehearsals they expressed their nervousness to actor James Grout who was also appearing in the show. He advised them to make some joke about the Royal presence. John, as always, had to be the spokesman. Grinning at the audience he said: 'Those in the cheap seats clap their hands.' Then looking up towards the Queen Mother in the Royal box he added, 'The rest of you just rattle your jewellery.'

Quite the most amazing thing during that first year was how everyone tried to jump on to the bandwagon. Members of Parliament asked silly questions in the House of Commons, the Conservative MP Edward Heath criticized the way they spoke, and religious leaders said all kinds of soft platitudes about them.

But through all the intellectualizing and taking of stances the clear-headedness of the Beatles themselves stuck out distinctively.

Perhaps they were not taken in by all the cant: or perhaps they were just too busy to realize what was happening to them.

John summed up the lunacy exactly when he told Maureen Cleave: 'We are the "now" sound. People try to pin labels on us, but I've never believed in any of that since I read that calypso was going to take England by storm about two years ago. It's all just good fun to us.' Commenting upon his art college background he was sardonically agreeable: 'It helps being intelligent I suppose, although I've met a few people in this business who aren't as thick as they look. On second thoughts I'd rather be thick and rich, than bright and otherwise.'

The Beatles' second album, *With the Beatles*, was the one that turned all the heads of the intellectuals. Now they had begun to explore the avenues of electronics and double tracking, and EMI were prepared to grant them more facilities at the Abbey Road studios. In those days John and Paul wrote 'eyeball to eyeball'. Of 'Little Child' John was to say: 'Paul and I wrote that as a throwaway for Ringo. If the songs were lousy we gave them to George or Ringo to sing. On the first album George sang "Do You Want to Know a Secret". It wasn't that we were trying to make him invisible, but simply that he had never written anything and he could only just sing. He could only just get his voice out of his throat. I encouraged him like mad. Of course he got a lot better didn't he? We knocked off "I Wanna Be Your Man" for the Rolling Stones after Brian had taken us down to a club in Richmond where they were playing. We let Ringo sing that one. "It Won't Be Long" and "Not a Second Time" were the ones that all the intellectual bullshit was written about. They were just chords like any other chords. We often used to find that Paul would write the choruses to songs and then not know where to go, and I would come up with the middle eight . . . the hook line. We actually wrote "From Me to You" in a van while we were touring around England. We nearly didn't do it because it was too bluesy, but by the time George Martin had finished scoring it with harmonica it was all right.'

The debt the Beatles owed to producer George Martin is enormous, and yet Martin has always been the first to shrug off all compliments which he feels should have been directed at the songwriters. It was Martin who scored virtually all the Beatle songs, from 'Yesterday' to 'Eleanor Rigby' and 'Strawberry Fields Forever', but he always saw himself as the interpreter of their music. In his book *All You Need is Ears* he wrote: 'Once you start being taught things your mind is channelled in a particular way. Paul and John didn't have that channelling, so they could think of things that I would have considered outrageous. I could admire them, but my musical training would have prevented me from thinking of them myself. I think, too, that the ability to write good tunes comes when someone is not fettered by rules and regulations of harmony and counterpoint. A tune is a one-finger thing, something you can whistle in the street. It doesn't depend upon great harmonies.' The ability to create good tunes was, he said, simply a gift.

America did not fall to the Beatles by accident. The success of their first appearances there in February 1964 was the result of a carefully orchestrated campaign organized by Brian Epstein and EMI's American subsidiary Capitol Records: it was a massive campaign of hype. On this rare occasion the hype was worth the effort. Once the Beatles had got their collective foot into the American door nothing could or did stop them.

While Beatlemania had been obsessing Britain, America had remained resolutely unimpressed. Indeed, Capitol had not even bothered to issue the first four Beatle singles in the States and smaller companies, Vee-Jay and Swann, had taken leases on them. But by the time of 'I Want to Hold Your Hand' all of Western Europe had fallen to the Beatles. Only then did Epstein manage to convince Capitol that they should put some real muscle into promotion. Accordingly, fifty thousand dollars was spent on publicity.

A few months earlier Ed Sullivan, the host of America's top Sunday evening television show, had been astonished by English fan reaction during a trip to London and he now agreed to book the Beatles on three successive Sunday night shows in February. They received top billing, but only half the fee usually given to the top spot. The money was unimportant. For three weeks in a row the Beatles were going to be exposed to nearly a third of the population of the United States.

To go with this promotion disc jockeys all over the States received tapes of Beatle interviews, Beatle pictures, and Beatle gimmicks, including Beatle wigs, stickers and buttons.

Then, just to make absolutely sure that no one in the whole of the United States could possibly be unaware of the imminent arrival of the Beatles, three thousand fans were hired to stage 'spontaneous' demonstrations at Kennedy Airport, and to scream with an ever-increasing hysteria as the Beatles' plane drew nearer to New York. The exercise went with an extraordinary precision, beyond Epstein's wildest dreams. 'I Want to Hold Your Hand' went to number one in the American charts within a month, and then the four of the group's previous British hits were re-released in the States in the wake of the hype. By March the Beatles occupied the top five places in the American Hot Hundred, with a couple of other records further down the Top Twenty.

Now a new happening was added to the Beatles' repertoire: the Beatle press conference. Wherever the Beatles appeared across America they would give press conferences before being whisked away and locked up inside their hotel rooms. The British press always flew with them and sent endless reports back home, but the American TV and newspaper men had to be content with simple questions and answers, opportunities for the four to show a jokey contempt for the banality of the questions. John, as always, took the lead.

'Does all the adulation from teenage girls affect you?' John was asked.

'No,' came the answer. 'Whenever I feel my head start to swell I look at Ringo and know perfectly well we're not supermen.'

'What excuse do you have for your collar-length hair?'

'It just grows out of my head.'

'Do you wear wigs?'

'If we do they must be the only ones with real dandruff.'

'How do you stand on the draft?'

'About five feet eleven inches.'

'How do you decide who sings the lead?'

'We just get together and the person who knows most words sings it.'

The banter with the press was never-ending. Generally the style was to take every question at completely face value and throw it back at the interviewer with a mock and a grin. It never failed. Quickly the four Beatles worked their press conferences into the form of an act, chipping backwards and forwards between themselves. They were, the newspapers said, like the Marx Brothers.

Before the Beatles nearly all rock stars had been humble and intimidated by the press. But the strength of the Beatle fellowship gave them a buoyant, cheeky optimism. On the plane over on that first trip all four of them felt some understandable signs of trepidation, worry in case they should fall flat on their faces. But John was later to tell *Rolling Stone* that he was certain that once America had seen the Beatles play they would be a success. 'We were really professional by the time we got to the States,' he said. 'We had learned the whole game . . . the British press are the toughest in the world. We could handle anything. I know on the plane over I was thinking "oh we won't make it" . . . but that's that side of me. We knew we would wipe 'em out if we could just get a grip . . . And then when we got here you were all walking around in fucking Bermuda shorts with Boston crew cuts and stuff on your teeth . . . the chicks looked like 1940s horses. There was no conception of dress or any of that jazz. We just thought "what an ugly race, what an ugly race".'

A year earlier the Beatles had helped change the physical appearance of British youth. Now America was to follow. Overnight long hair became fashionable. By the end of 1964 John Lennon's gang stretched all around the world. We were all

Quarrymen then. There were no more peaks to be scaled. 'The only thing left for us to do now is to die,' said John.

Between 1964 and 1966 the Beatles toured the world almost constantly, doing twenty-minute shows and televised press conferences, feeling like caged animals inside their rooms while the legions of fans mobbed the hotels in which they were staying. The Beatle women always stayed at home.

'We were,' said John, 'like kings of the jungle. Like Caesars.' Everything they wanted, with the exception of their freedom from public perusal, was granted to them, every kind of physical gratification was lavished on them. Brian Epstein was a promoter and diplomat extraordinary. Somehow the Beatles' wholesome image was never allowed to falter. When asked for his opinion on the Vietnam War, John would bite his tongue and make some vague comment about being against all war.

Gradually the Lennon lip, the cheekiness, the recklessness was being emasculated. He was still funny, still the clown, but the endless shaking of hands with local dignitaries and their daughters was suffocating. The man who had always hated the establishment, who had hated the discipline of school uniform, was now the darling of society, wearing neat little Beatle uniforms, and being polite to the sort of self-important people he had always loathed. He would later claim that he only went along with it because Paul and Brian wanted him to. But that was an excuse for his own guilt at selling out. John went along with everything because he wanted to be rich and famous. When the Beatles first became successful they spoke endlessly about the prospects of becoming rich. When they got rich they wanted to be richer. This is no criticism. They all realized early that wealth meant power. Later John was to use his wealth and fame in a variety of idiosyncratic ways. But first he had to swallow his own ego.

Of course there were moments when that ego stuck firmly in his throat, as, for example, the occasion at the British Embassy in Washington when some silly socialite ('some bloody animal', said John) cut off a lock of Ringo's hair. Lennon, followed by his gang, roared out of the reception under a cloud of blue anger.

Quickly the world became an anonymous place to the Beatles during those days of constant touring. They criss-crossed Europe, the Far East, Australia, America and Canada as well as Britain. But they saw hardly anything other than an endless number of fan-decked airport terminals and the interiors of hotel suites. Even there they would be so mobbed by their entourage that they would eventually all end up in a bathroom together, usually smoking a joint. Their view of the world was unique. Never before in history had any group of people been so famous, so loved by so many, so isolated from everyday life. They were treated like royalty, but they had not the grounding to know how to behave as royalty. That they were ever to emerge with their sanity intact from the lunacy of Beatlemania is extraordinary. That they also managed to be creative under the most manic of circumstances was a credit to their ability as musicians. Yet some of their best songs were written under the most extreme kind of pressure, the pressure to make their every record better than the preceding one.

In March 1964 the sixth Beatles single 'Can't Buy Me Love' was released with an advance order of more than a million copies in Britain alone. John's song 'You Can't Do That' was on the flip side. 'That was my attempt at being Wilson Pickett,' he said.

A few days later filming began on *A Hard Day's Night*, a grainy, zany semi-documentary in which director Dick Lester captured well the claustrophobia of Beatle life. The style of the film was another inspired move. In America Elvis was making films like *Paradise Hawaiian Style*, coppertanned, mindless escapist junk. In Britain the Beatles were capturing the excitement of the moment. As though this were not enough John's first book *In His Own Write* was published to respectable, if slightly patronizing reviews from literary critics at the end of that month. Basically, *In His Own Write* was a continuation of the style of writing John had been practising from childhood – silly poems of black comedy, grotesque cartoons and short, pun-laden stories. By the end of the year the book had sold 300,000 copies, mainly to people who had probably never before bought a hardback book in their entire lives. What *In His Own Write* was to establish beyond doubt was that behind the lovable mop-top image there was a truly original mind. The drawings were compared with Thurber and Steinberg, the endless wordplay with Stanley Unwin, Spike Milligan, Lewis Carroll and James Joyce, and the black menace which hung over so much of the text with Harold Pinter and Edward Lear. (A year later a second book, *A Spaniard in the Works*, was published, although with rather less acclaim.)

More tours and more records followed. In an attempt to escape the hysteria of London John now bought his first large house, Kenwood, in the stockbroker belt of St George's Hill Estate near Weybridge in Surrey. But it was hardly ever to be a home for him. Cynthia moved in with Julian, but John was usually away touring, or locked in the Abbey Road recording studios. Shopping for any of the Beatles had become virtually impossible, so things were ordered at whim, delivered and discarded. In many respects John's house was ridiculous, a large mock-Tudor place, with a pool and a small recording studio. He had more money than he knew what to do with, but at that time he never had the opportunity to work out what he really wanted out of life. Like the others he had become a prisoner of his own fame.

Kenwood was a big mistake for John, because by nature he was a city man. As he said later he needed 'to be somewhere to watch the wheels go round and round'. But it was far safer for Cynthia and Julian to live way out in a remote part of the rich suburbs, where they would be less disturbed by the constant frenzy.

None of this affected the music, however. The Lennon and McCartney partnership was now writing at speed, but writing well. Their music was still rock and roll, but it was becoming more distinctive with every album. In 1965 they changed direction with the albums *Help!* and *Rubber Soul*. They had gone as far as possible with the four-man line-up and double tracking, and now additional musicians began to be introduced to augment their sound. For Paul's song 'Yesterday' George Martin suggested a string quartet. The record was released as a Beatles track, but the only Beatle involved in it was Paul. John did not help write it, and none of the Beatles played on it. At the same time John was becoming more and more interested in making his lyrics more intelligent. At first he and Paul had written about boy-girl relationships because that was the way all the other writers did. Now John wanted to be more personal, and being very impressed by Bob Dylan (he even began to sing like him for a while) he began to write about his moods. 'I'm a Loser' was typical: 'Although I laugh and I act like a clown, beneath this mask I am wearing a frown.' 'Norwegian Wood' was a song about an extra-marital affair which he was trying to disguise from Cynthia.

The *Rubber Soul* sessions of 1965 produced some of the best Beatle tracks ever recorded, particularly John's autobiographical 'In My Life', on which George Martin played an Elizabethan piano solo, and the beautiful song 'Girl': 'Is there anybody going to listen to my story, All about the girl who came to stay.' It was John's poetry to a fantasy girl, a sad reflection upon the unevenness of love: 'When I think of all the times I've tried so hard to leave her, She will turn to me and start to cry. Then she promises the world to me and I believe her, After all this time I don't know why.'

John always considered 'Girl' to be one of his best songs. But although all Beatle records were accepted with relish by the fans John was never slow to criticize his own early work, or be flippantly casual about it. Of 'I Feel Fine' he was dismissive: 'I wrote it in the studio around a riff.' About 'Yes It Is', which was the flip side of 'Ticket to Ride', he was brutal to himself: 'That was me trying to write "This Boy" again. Same harmony, same chords and double-dutch words. It was embarrassing – "if you wear red tonight", Jesus Christ!' Of 'It's Only Love' he was even more ashamed: 'That was the most embarrassing thing I ever wrote. Everything rhymed. The lyrics were disgusting. Even then I was so ashamed I could hardly sing them. That must be the worst thing I ever wrote. Well actually I could say that about quite a few of them come to think of it.' One song he particularly disliked was 'Run For Your Life' which ended the *Rubber Soul* album. It was a song he knocked off in a hurry because they needed something to finish the album, and he openly admitted to pinching a line from Elvis Presley's 'Baby Let's Play House' ('I'd rather see you dead little girl than to be with another man'). To the listeners it was a good up-beat Beatles record. But later John was to hate its macho sentiments. 'I was going through my fat Elvis period in those days,' he would say later, looking at pictures of himself with horror.

Although Cynthia and Julian were being kept very much in the background one member of the Lennon family was determined to put himself as far in the foreground as possible. That was, of course, long-lost father Freddie who, one night, turned up at John's Weybridge house with a reporter from the *Daily Express*. Characteristically, John did not make him welcome on that first occasion but, being John, he was always a soft touch, and when Freddie persisted John did in fact have some sort of relationship with his errant father. Freddie had not had a particularly exciting life, but he had the gift of the gab. John did not exactly like him, but for a short time he put up with him, gave him money and, contrary to legend, did allow him into the house. Eventually Freddie was to marry one of the Apple secretaries and have another son. He died of cancer in 1977.

By 1965 the Beatles had won every possible kind of musical accolade (Aaron Copland and Leonard Bernstein considered Lennon and McCartney serious modern composers), and they were the darlings of the critics. Then in June 1965 Labour Prime Minister Harold Wilson made them the darlings of the establishment when it was announced that the four Beatles had been awarded the MBE. John was embarrassed by the idea. 'If the Palace had bothered to read what I thought about Royalty they would never have allowed it,' he said later. 'I didn't want to accept it, but I could hardly refuse when the other three wanted theirs. So I allowed myself to be talked into it.' It is unlikely that anyone had to talk very hard. In those days John went along with majority decisions on nearly everything. He was too lazy to argue. There is a well-known, but totally untrue story, that John smoked a joint in a bathroom at Buckingham Palace. John told that to a French reporter shortly after the investiture, but he was lying. It was just a little boast of bravado, which he later regretted. 'We'd have been far too scared to do anything like that,' he said.

For three years the Beatles had charmed lives. There were minor rows, of course, as when protocol was upset during a visit to the Governor's Mansion in Nassau, and riots when, on a mis-understanding the Beatles were said to have deliberately snubbed the President of the Philippines ('I didn't know they even had a President,' said John testily), but their long predicted come-uppance and fall from grace never materialized. Then in March 1966 John gave a characteristically frank interview to the *Evening Standard*'s Maureen Cleave. Maureen had been writing about the Beatles since January 1963, when she had written the first major piece to appear in any large circulation newspaper. She was particularly close to John so it was ironical that it was one of her articles that was to set loose the first of the 'hate Lennon' campaigns.

During the interview Maureen asked John for his views on religion. He said: 'Christianity will go. It will vanish and shrink. I needn't argue about that. I'm right and I will be proved right. We're more popular than Jesus now. I don't know which will go first – rock and roll or Christianity. Jesus was all right but his disciples were thick and ordinary. It's them twisting it that ruins it for me.'

When this interview was published in relatively sophisticated London no one noticed anything particularly amiss. It was merely an interesting point, well articulated. Besides it was demonstrably true that the Beatles were more popular than Jesus with young people at that particular moment. But when the interview was reprinted in an American fan magazine called *Dateline* on the eve of what was to be the Beatles' final tour of America a frenzy of hate and animosity hit the group. There were anti-Beatle rallies and outraged Church leaders condemned Lennon from the pulpit. The Grand Dragon of the Ku Klux Klan in South Carolina burned a Beatles record on a cross, radio stations banned their records, and one Texas station held a public burning of Beatles records.

Epstein and the other Beatles were genuinely concerned about their safety should they go through with their forthcoming tour. Maureen Cleave graciously and loyally suggested to John that he might say he had been misquoted. He refused. He had meant what he said. Finally he went before television news cameras and explained that he had not been putting down Christ or religion, but simply making an observation. It was in no way an apology, but for once the easy jokes had left him: the arrogance was no longer there. He looked beaten by the system. He was being destroyed by the very fact that as a Beatle he was no longer able to say what he thought about anything without it being misconstrued. He was still only twenty-five and the effort of touring and keeping up a bland, merry, clowning image year after year was crippling him mentally. He admitted that he was sorry that he had made the statement. He told a reporter: 'I'm not anti-God, anti-Christ or anti-religion. I was not saying that we are greater or better than Jesus. I believe in God, but not as one thing, not as an old man in the sky . . . I wasn't saying that the Beatles are better than God or Jesus. I used *Beatles* because it's easy for me to talk about Beatles. I could have said TV or the cinema or anything popular and I would have got away with it.'

In another interview he said: 'I never meant it to be a lousy anti-religious thing. Christianity just seems to me to be shrinking, to be losing contact. It's only in the last two years that I – all the Beatles – have begun looking for something else. We live in a moving hot-house. We've been mushroom-grown, forced to grow up a bit quick, like having thirty- to forty-year-old heads in twenty-year-old bodies.'

Whether or not his explanation satisfied the blinkered Christian hysterics, the Beatles once again toured America with the same rapturous welcomes wherever they appeared. If any of the Bible

20. The Maharishi 'made a fool of everyone', said John when he arrived back in April 1968 from meditating in the Himalayas, but by then he had provided thousands of newspaper headlines and cartoons. In case you don't recognize him, John is sitting alongside Cynthia on the right-hand side of the second row. Next to John is Beatle roadie, Mal Evans, who was later shot dead by the Los Angeles police during a misunderstanding.

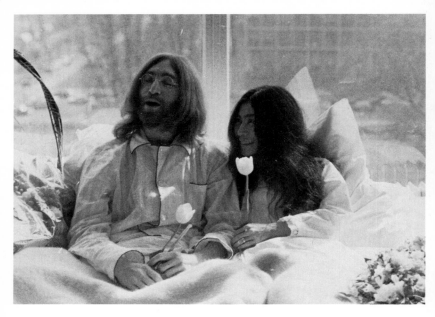

21. The Amsterdam Bed-in of 1969. 'We'll stay in bed for a week,' said John. It was all in the name of peace.

22. Another Yoko-inspired event was Bagism in April 1969. The public was becoming increasingly hostile and confused.

23. The Lennons' ability to attract publicity drew all kinds of people to them, including the parents of James Hanratty who had been hanged eight years earlier for a murder which his parents always claimed he did not commit. The occasion was the Royal Première of Ringo's film *Magic Christian* in 1969.

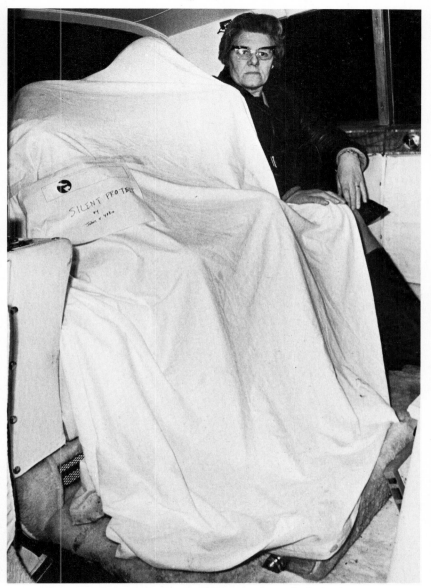

24. Bagism for Hanratty. Was that really John and Yoko in the bag?

25. The Lennons' 1969 Christmas peace campaign, War Is Over, was turned into a hit record, 'Happy Christmas, War Is Over', two years later. It became a big hit again in December 1980.

26. John attracted some very dubious friends, of whom Michael X, later hanged for murder in the West Indies, was by far the most unsavoury.

27. John even took his People for Peace message on to the BBC's programme *Top of the Pops*, when he sang 'Instant Karma'.

28. John and Yoko at an anti-war rally in New York in 1972.

Belt lunatics who had condemned Lennon had thought about it for one moment, the success of that final tour which ended in Candlestick Park, San Francisco, on August 29 was a vindication of everything. In 1966 the Beatles definitely were bigger than Christ among the young people of America, for better or for worse. But it hardly mattered any more. The days of touring were over. There was simply no point in going on.

'What else could we do?' asked John. 'Make more money? Play bigger concerts? Go on longer tours? There was no pleasure in playing any more, not like in the old days.' The strain of being the lovable mop-tops had reached breaking point. In another interview he said: 'It was a complete oppression for us. I mean we had to go through humiliation upon humiliation with the middle classes and showbiz and Lord Mayors and all that. They were so condescending and so stupid. Everybody was trying to use us. It was a special humiliation for me because I could never keep my mouth shut and I'd always have to be drunk or pilled to counteract this pressure. It was really hell.'

One way out of the hell for him and the other Beatles was an increasing interest in drugs. Ever since the Hamburg days when John had taken to gulping down handfuls of Preludin to keep awake he had had more than a passing interest in dope. By 1966 the new craze was acid – LSD, the hallucinogen which the CIA had helped develop for their own nefarious ends and which considerable numbers of young people were to turn to in the late sixties. Acid has often been described as a mind expanding drug – but this is a misleading description. What acid does is to alter the individual's perception to a considerable degree. It can be an ecstatic experience and it can be terrifying. In the mid and late sixties people who were 'into acid' became virtually missionaries to their own cause, notably Dr Timothy Leary, a clinical psychologist who was to develop a whole philosophy for the era based on the essays contained in his book *The Politics of Ecstasy*. Leary's acid crusade was condemned by all strata of medical opinion and there is no doubt that LSD can have harmful effects upon the brain cells, but in the mid-sixties, when psychedelia and illustration were everything, the warnings of the wary went unheeded.

For John Lennon LSD came as something of a shock. A dentist friend ('a middle-class London swinger, you know the sort of people George hangs out with') slipped it into his coffee when he and George with their wives were at dinner. After that the evening turned into pure surrealism. The two couples visited the then fashionable Ad Lib club in London's West End, and then, driving at ten miles an hour, they all made it back to George's house in Esher, Surrey. For John it was frightening, but it was also tempting. The world of Lewis Carroll had come real in his life. For a month or two he considered what had happened to him, and then during a tour of America he went to a Hollywood party and took some more deliberately. The party was full of Beatle groupies like Peter Fonda and the Byrds, and also reporters, and John, George and Ringo who had all taken acid were terrified in case the British journalists present should notice the state they were in. During the party Peter Fonda kept saying, 'I know what it's like to be dead . . .' because he was tripping out also. In the end the whole experience turned into the song 'She Said, She Said', one of the most powerful tracks on *Revolver*, the only Beatles album of 1966. ('She said, "I know what it's like to be dead."')

But before *Revolver* was released there was to be one further single, 'Paperback Writer', which was mainly by Paul, plus 'Rain', for which John was mainly responsible. It was not one of the Beatles' best records, but there was an amusing anecdote about the recording of 'Rain'. Apparently when John got home from the studios, rather the worse for dope one night, he decided to play 'Rain' in his home studio, where he often experimented on the ten attached Brunel tape recorders he had had installed. Inadvertently he put the tape on back to front and found himself listening to the song backwards. So bemused was he by what he heard that it took him some little time to work out what had gone wrong. When he discovered his mistake he decided to use the device on the end of the record – which explains why at the end of 'Rain' the music suddenly goes into reverse. Later John's little studio was to provide whole albums of barely recognizable sounds.

Revolver was the album of new directions. *Rubber Soul* had taken the Beatles to the limit of rock and roll. Now they were to begin shaking a cultural kaleidoscope.

The most outstanding track on *Revolver* was Paul's song 'Eleanor Rigby'. John always claimed to have written half of the lyrics ('wearing a face that she keeps in a jar by the door' seems particularly Lennonesque) but he was always fulsome in his praise of Paul's genius for having conceived the song in the first place, and for encouraging producer George Martin to score it in the style of Haydn. The two next-best tracks were also by Paul: 'For No One' and 'Here, There and Everywhere'. Again John praised them very highly, even when later he and Paul fell out. 'Yellow Submarine', on which they collaborated more fully, has now become a much-loved nursery rhyme. The Beatles dressed up a simple song with wit and funny sounds, but it was never more than a throwaway children's song which was given to Ringo to sing. Little children always liked Ringo best.

John's contribution to ,*Revolver* was largely disappointing, but there were forceful intimations of the way his music was developing. 'I'm Only Sleeping' ('Everybody seems to think I'm lazy, I don't mind I think they're crazy, Running everywhere at such a speed, 'til they find there's no need') was a theme he was to take up again fourteen years later for his last album with one of his best-ever songs, 'Watching the Wheels', in which he simply described the contentment of sitting back and watching the world go by. As has often been observed John had an immense capacity for sleeping and daydreaming.

The last track on *Revolver* was the psychedelically inspired 'Tomorrow Never Knows'. In many ways it could be seen as a rehearsal for 'Strawberry Fields Forever' and 'I Am the Walrus', in that it appeared to be an invitation to join him in a hallucinatory journey. 'Turn off your mind relax and float down stream,' he sings, taking lines from the Tibetan Book of the Dead, which

Timothy Leary had pointed in his direction. As a melody it barely rose above a dirge and John was always unsatisfied with the way it was recorded. He said: 'Often the backing I think of never comes off. With "Tomorrow Never Knows" I had imagined in my head that in the background you would hear thousands of monks chanting. That was impractical of course and we did something different. I should have tried to get nearer to my original idea, because that was what I really wanted.'

By the time of *Revolver* all four Beatles had developed extraordinarily as musicians. At first George Martin had been the producer in that his function was to get them to shape their songs and then get a good mix on tape. By 1966 he was being used more as an arranger. Since none of the Beatles could read or write music they would have to sing, hum or play on guitar the ideas they had in their minds and then ask Martin to try and capture that sound with other instruments. It was often a laborious process of trial and error, as George Martin tried to translate into the language of trained musicians the sounds which Lennon and McCartney wanted. Martin was obviously closer to Paul than he was to John because the sounds Paul wanted on his songs were often inspired by the classical records he was encouraged to listen to by his girlfriend of the time, actress Jane Asher. How George Martin was supposed to capture the sound of thousands of Tibetan monks in a small studio in Abbey Road was another matter altogether.

In his attempts to get closer to the Beatles musically Martin, an accomplished oboist, even took up learning the guitar, but quickly forgot the idea when he realized that Lennon and McCartney were mastering the piano more quickly than he could the guitar. At the beginning of their careers John and Paul would always write with their guitars, but as their proficiency with the piano progressed their awareness of expression was automatically widened. It is inconceivable that Paul could ever have written 'Let It Be', or John have written 'Imagine', without having mastered the piano.

'In the old days Paul and I just used to write and write all the time,' said John. 'But later on I only wrote when I felt I had something to write about, or when I was particularly inspired. I could churn out a million songs like the early ones if I wanted to. But I don't want to any more. That sort of writing brings me down.

'Proper writing is never easy. I try to write in all kinds of combinations, at the piano or at the guitar, or just play around with a phrase that's going through my head. Mainly it's torture if I'm trying too hard.

'I try not to write for quite long periods because I don't want to be panicked into it, then when I haven't done anything for a while I get this awful guilt and I begin to think "Oh Christ, I can't write any more". So I have to get on with it and then go through the torture of recording. Then when I finish I get disappointed because I haven't quite captured what I was trying to do. I suppose I sometimes find it pretty hard to live up to being John Lennon.'

With the days of touring over all the Beatles were forced to begin reassessing their lives. Paul began to compose incidental music for the Boulting Brothers film *The Family Way*, George immersed himself in learning the sitar from Ravi Shankar, and in developing his interest in Indian mysticism, and John went off to Spain to try his hand at straight acting in Dick Lester's film *How I Won the War*. All through Beatlemania John had kept silent about his feelings about the war in Vietnam. Now Dick Lester was giving him the opportunity to help make an anti-war statement. But he did not enjoy filming. He was bored for much of the time, and he quickly realized that acting did not take the place of music in his life. But his real problem lay in the fact that he did not know what to do with his life any more. Ever since leaving school he had been playing regularly in a band. Now the band had got too big to play. He needed a new direction.

A Year in the Life
of the Walrus
and the Egg Man

There never was a year quite like 1967. To some people it was the year when popular music reached a pinnacle of creativity; to many others it was a time when the whole world suddenly became very, very silly. To John Lennon it was a time of massive dosages of LSD (he later told *Rolling Stone*, 'I must have had a thousand trips. I used to eat it all the time'), of *Sergeant Pepper*, and of a new fascination with all things mystic. It was also the year in which he turned his recurrent 'Three Blind Mice' theme into a world anthem which caught perfectly the mood of the moment – 'All You Need is Love', the song the Beatles first sang before an audience of over 150 million people in the first intercontinental satellite telethon, *Our World*.

Nineteen sixty-seven was also a period of quicksilver changes in which the public's love affair with the Beatles continually altered perspective – from blind adoration to bewildered admiration, to curiosity, and, finally, by the end of the year, to open derision after the critical failure of their *Magical Mystery Tour* television film.

But most of all 1967 will be remembered for the Indian summer, when overnight a million hippies in bells, beads and kaftans appeared in cities of the world, apparently floating on a marijuana cloud which seemed to stretch all the way from the Monterey Pop Festival to San Francisco and on throughout America, Europe and Asia to the foothills of Nepal. It was like a psychedelically painted caravan of dreams which rolled around the world accompanied musically by the soaring creativity of *Sergeant Pepper's Lonely Hearts Club Band.* In 1963 the emergence of the Beatles had changed the course of rock and roll music; now, in 1967, rock music graduated with honours as Lennon's verbal gobbledegook and black cartoons found their way from his books on to the records in songs which dazzled with surrealistic images and were Aladdin's caves of allusion and illusion.

It was also the year in which Brian Epstein was found dead from an accidental drugs overdose in his London flat, when the Maharishi 'made a fool of everyone' (according to the lyrics of 'Sexy Sadie' which a disillusioned John later wrote about the Maharishi), and when John Lennon sponsored an exhibition by an ambitious Japanese avant-garde artiste called Yoko Ono at London's Lisson Gallery.

By the spring of 1967 John Lennon was living in mock-Tudor splendour on the vastly expensive St George's Hill Estate in Weybridge, Surrey, and had become what he had always despised, and always would – a suburban family man. He was twenty-six years old, was one of the most famous people ever to have lived, had appeared in three films, published two books and written and sung some of the world's best-known songs; and, in the eyes of everyone apart from his accountant, he was vastly rich. He was also becoming increasingly bored. Fame and wealth had bought him time, but they had also placed him in an alien culture. During the years of touring there had been little time to sit and think. Now there was little else to do but sit and think. The bleak sentiments of his song 'Nowhere Man' (admittedly written two years earlier) now fitted his mood exactly. He had become the 'real nowhere man, sitting in his Nowhere Land, making all his nowhere plans for nobody'. In a sense he was suffering a retreat into the loneliness of childhood. As Ringo, who lived just down the road, said at the time: 'Sometimes I go up to John's house to play with his toys, and sometimes he comes down here to play with mine.'

In the spring of that year the double-sided hit, 'Penny Lane' (mainly by Paul) and 'Strawberry Fields Forever' (John), was released. Although both songs were evocations of childhood, the difference between Paul's interpretation and John's was immense. Paul always liked to write little stories into his songs – about the fireman, the barber and the nurse in this case. But John was now moving into vocal streams of consciousness. A lot of the lyrics of 'Strawberry Fields' is almost meaningless, but one line stands out like a blade among the morass of moogs, cellos and changing rhythms. 'Living is easy with eyes closed, misunderstanding all you see,' wrote John, before descending into a hallucinatory ramble.

This was quite the most bizarre Beatle record so far and immediately spurred all kinds of pseuds and crackpots to launch theories about their interpretation. The words were mainly just random phrases which sounded good, but John enjoyed the controversy. It flattered his ego to be considered the genius he thought he was, even if at that time the genius could only articulate itself with the help of a little acid and George Martin's electronic wizardry and recording expertise which spliced together two separate takes, one of which was speeded up to put it in a different key.

Later, when John tried to explain the genesis of 'Strawberry Fields Forever' he would talk about the Salvation Army School behind Auntie Mimi's house in Menlove Road, Liverpool, where he went as a child to see the band play at garden parties; and he would then attempt to explain the lyrics in terms of hiding his real meanings behind self-conscious poetry. But it has to be possible that eventually he, like so many others, succumbed to the temptation to read more into his lyrics than had been originally intended. While one side of him derided the intellectualizing which went on around him, his other, frustrated intellectual side, relished it.

Still, while 'Strawberry Fields Forever' may not have been the best music John Lennon was ever to compose, it fitted to perfection the ever-widening horizons of popular music in 1967. It is a dreamy meandering song to which any interpretation can be, and has been, given. John never said 'Paul is dead' at the end of the track; he said 'Cranberry Sauce'. But in the late sixties every nonsense Beatle line came with its college of apostles and apologists.

Most of the spring and early summer of 1967 was taken up with the production and release of the *Sergeant Pepper* album. As always Paul was the busy, energetic one, but on this album it was John's imagery which was to baffle and win the admiration of the critics. By now, however, there had been a remarkable shift in public attitudes towards the Beatles. Even Paul had now admitted to the press to having tried LSD and John's line in 'A Day in the Life', 'I'd love to turn you on', won him worldwide reprobation from generations of people who saw him as a Pied Piper of drugs.

In retrospect the worriers may have had half a point. Ever since the Beatles had been so firmly clasped to the bosom of the establishment, their every antic had been feasted by the press as another example of the lovable mop-tops' exuberance, and the youth of the world had been encouraged to note their industry, shampooed cleanliness and apparent decency. So when these same four young men decided, with the waning influence of Brian Epstein, to speak out for themselves, and were seen to be endorsing ways of life which many considered to be of dubious social value, huge cracks suddenly appeared in the smiling faces of welcome which had been virtually the Beatles' only view of the world during the past five years.

Sergeant Pepper was not, in my opinion, the Beatles' finest creation, but because of its timing, and the remarkable prescience which the Beatles showed for public changes of mood, it was a landmark in popular music . . . a milestone from which everyone interested in music could chart his course. Considering that it was recorded fairly simply on a four-track console at EMI's Abbey Road studio (most groups today use at least sixteen tracks for the simplest of sessions) it is certainly a monument to the electronic expertise of George Martin. Everything about *Sergeant Pepper* was heady and extravagant, from the flower-power cover with its collections of cut-outs and famous faces, to the cost of the four months' recording sessions (£25,000 – an astronomical sum in those days; the whole of the Beatles' first album had been recorded in a single day for just £400).

The songs on *Sergeant Pepper* displayed a new breadth of vision in the work of John and Paul. John may have laughed off 'Being for the Benefit of Mr Kite' as a complete pinch because he had taken virtually every line from a poster he picked up in an antique shop, but he was secretly proud of his ability to turn something so unlikely into a very clever, poetic and popular song, and he kept the original poster framed on the kitchen wall, first at Weybridge and later at his house in Tittenhurst Park, Ascot.

At the time even the most kindly and sympathetic of reviewers (this one included) was rather sceptical about his assertion that the initial letters to 'Lucy in the Sky with Diamonds' referred not to LSD but to a playgroup painting brought home by the four-year-old Julian, but John's insistence over the years that the association was totally coincidental was ultimately convincing. While Paul brought the stronger melodic lines and humour to the album with 'When I'm Sixty-Four', 'With a Little Help from My Friends' and 'She's Leaving Home' (with all of which John helped), it was John's song (with a middle section from Paul) 'A Day in the Life' which was the most innovative track, the lyrics being mostly taken from odd lines in the *Daily Mail* or references to John's part in the film *How I Won the War*, while the total arrangement had an almost ecclesiastical grandiloquence about it. For me it is the most ambitious track the Beatles ever recorded, a perfect fusion of the separate but equal weights of Lennon and McCartney.

When *Sergeant Pepper* was released in May there was a massive heady excitement with radio stations competing with each other to be the first to play it. Despite a panning review in the *New York Times* it was dazzlingly successful. Rock and roll music had shown a new literacy. You could not dance to Sergeant Pepper: you simply had to listen. 'Listen to the words, man,' Bob Dylan had urged Lennon three years earlier when playing him an acetate of his latest songs. 'I never listen to words,' John had replied, probably lying a little, but being dismissive of lyrics nevertheless. Now he showed that not only did he listen: he could write better, more tormented, wittier lyrics than any of his contemporaries. He nailed the flower-power hedonism of that summer and put it on to black vinyl. Whenever and wherever *Sergeant Pepper* is played today the time it evokes is always the same: the Indian summer of 1967.

Then almost before anyone was ready for it the Beatles were back in the studios at Abbey Road again, but this time in party spirit, with their wives, girlfriends, balloons and television cameras for the transmission of the British section of the worldwide television link-up, *Our World*. When first approached the Beatles had been unsure of whether they wanted to take part, but the possibility of the greatest single exposure in history for a new record was too good an opportunity to be ignored. And so, chewing gum nervously, John Lennon introduced the world to 'All You Need is Love' – cheating slightly since the programme was intended to be live, and the Beatles were actually miming to a recording already made specially for the show. It was another masterstroke of fitting the song to the moment, and an example of how adept John was becoming at producing slogans (instead of philosophies?) to measure, stealing a few bars for the opening from the international song of brotherhood 'The Marseillaise' and ending on a wryly cynical note with the chorus of 'She Loves You' being heard mockingly over the fade-out. By now the Beatles could afford to mock everything and everyone: even themselves. They had become four giants who bestrode the world. The pressure from all sides was unrelenting; and, only feeling secure in the presence of each other, all four, plus entourage, went off to Greece on holiday, while the residents of St George's Hill Estate fumed about the psychedelically painted caravan that John had parked on his front lawn. Some people would never understand.

Week by week that summer London seemed to become more and

more like an Indian bazaar. If someone had said that there were tangerine trees under marmalade skies in Hyde Park would anyone under the age of thirty have doubted it? Streets and subways jingled to the sound of bells, girls smiled behind kaleidoscope eyes (no one had the audacity to ask why they were smiling) and the florists' shops enjoyed a boom like never before. And then to top it all the giggling guru, better, though not so accurately, known as the Maharishi Mahesh Yogi, gave a series of public lectures in the Hilton Hotel on the benefits to be obtained from his form of transcendental meditation.

At George Harrison's suggestion John and Paul, together with Paul's brother, Mike McGear, went along to hear the wisdom of the holy man. John, as usual, had slightly ambivalent feelings about the whole thing. Partly embarrassed about being there at all before two thousand paying onlookers he quipped to Mike McGear: 'What's he going to do, tell a few jokes or sing a few songs?'

As it turned out the Maharishi did neither, but smiled and soothed away all doubts. After a private audience with the man the sceptics were convinced of the mystical benefits to be found in meditation and a week later found themselves boarding a train for Bangor, North Wales, along with Mick Jagger and Marianne Faithfull. Poor Cynthia Lennon broke into tears when a policeman barred her way and she missed the train. John was off to delve into the mysteries of the East and she had been left behind.

How much John and his friends might have seen through the Maharishi during that weekend in Bangor will always be impossible to tell, because on the Sunday afternoon their weekend of meditational instruction was rudely cut short. The body of Brian Epstein had been found in his London flat. He had died from a quite massive overdose of sleeping pills. There was no particular mystery around his death. The coroner was later convinced that death was accidental. But his death was symptomatic of the way the Beatles' affairs had been going. For months Epstein had found himself increasingly redundant to their schemes. No one, for instance, invited him to spend the weekend with the Maharishi. When the days of touring ended Epstein felt that the Beatles no longer needed him as their promoter. They now needed a dynamic business manager, and in that role he had never been very successful. The loneliness forced upon Epstein, partly by his homosexuality, and partly by the nagging view that he no longer had a function, tormented him into states of sleepless depression. Then, one lonely weekend when the boys he loved so much had gone off without him, he sank into a deep depression and, finding sleep impossible, began to increase his dose of Carbitral. After three days that dosage became fatal.

As the Beatles left Bangor to return to London by car that Sunday evening, the tortured face of John Lennon blinked uncomprehendingly into television news cameras as reporters asked for his instant response. He mouthed some platitudes about not being able to believe what had happened. But inside himself, he was later to admit, he was scared. Years later he told *Rolling Stone*: 'I knew that we were in trouble then. I didn't really have any misconceptions about our ability to do anything other than play music. I thought, "We've fucking had it." '

Despite what Brian Epstein may have felt in his depression John knew that he was not yet redundant to their needs. The Beatles still needed his soothing, administering ways to hold them together, to save them from each other.

'Roll up for the mystery tour, roll up,' began the song, and thus began the Beatles' first venture without a manager. Earlier in the year John had talked about making a new film with the Beatles following his disillusionment with straight acting in *How I Won the War*, and the Beatles' wholesale disappointment with *Help!* in which, they said, they felt like extras. Now they wanted to do everything themselves, using technicians in the way that they used them when making records. The fact that not one of them had any experience in film direction or production bothered them not at all.

'We'll do it without a director, perhaps even without a

85

scriptwriter,' said John. 'We'll play ourselves – not as a group, but as individuals – and it will grow as we go along.'

And that was exactly what they did – although it didn't actually work out in a way that any of them had planned. Perhaps as a diversion from grieving over the death of Epstein, *Magical Mystery Tour* was set up within a month of his funeral. One bright morning in September a gaily festooned coach full of extras, camera technicians and Paul McCartney set off from London's Marylebone Road for Cornwall by way of Weybridge, Surrey, where it picked up the three other members of the group and their assorted retinues.

By any standards of film-making it was a bizarre way to begin a production. Perhaps a small, unknown group in the hands of a capable director and a good script could have turned out a masterpiece of a film. But the Beatles were neither small nor unknown. And now their very celebrity worked against them as they set off on their adventure accompanied by eager eccentrics such as Ivor Cutler, a dwarf, a fat lady, a couple of starlets, and a procession of reporters who tailed the bizarrely decorated coach down through southern England. No action of the Beatles escaped massive public interest and by the second day the queue of cars bearing press and fans stretched back half a mile, winding curiously across the Devonshire moors. On board, meanwhile, a little filming and much discussion of the film went on. At lunchtime the inevitable happened on a humpback bridge on the road to Widdicombe Fair. The coach became jammed. It couldn't go forward and it couldn't reverse out. The press loved it. Inside, trapped as the Beatles had so often been before, John watched with a kind of bored amusement. He appeared to have little interest in the film and Paul was taking over the direction even as early as this. Within a month of Brian Epstein's death, it was Paul who was dictating to the others the way he felt things ought to go. And because John was bored, probably a little dopey (in the literal sense) and certainly lazy he allowed it to happen. Someone had to lead the Beatles, and Paul had the energy and enthusiasm for it.

By the time the Magical Mystery coach, now badly scratched on both sides and a couple of inches slimmer, reached Newquay in Cornwall, it had become obvious that the Beatles were never going to be able to make the film they had planned. The holiday resort had been enjoying a quiet, sunny September season before the Beatles and their following hit the town. Suddenly everywhere was chaos. Paul, in his Fair Isle pullover, walked about energetically talking to associate producer Gavrik Losey about what should be done, George sat cross-legged on a headland and meditated (or perhaps he just sat!), Ringo stayed in the hotel and joked with the press, and John... well John was there somewhere, making the odd joke, dressed up like the most eccentric of English holidaymakers in a suit and trilby and peering sardonically through his glasses at the lunacy surrounding him. At that moment he reminded me of a man trapped inside a glass booth who sees the world going on all around him, but is somehow not part of that world.

After one week's filming, done mainly in the coach since it was virtually impossible for the Beatles ever to get out of it, location shooting was abandoned and the crew returned to London to complete the venture at Shepperton Studios.

In October *How I Won the War* opened to generally good notices, although it was widely accepted that John's acting left something to be desired. He did not seem to care. He had already decided that acting was a drag and had no wish to appear in any more films. His interest in this particular movie had been sparked by the subject matter: it was a black anti-war comedy. He said: 'I hate war. If there is another war I won't fight and I'll try to tell all the youngsters not to fight either. I hate all the sham...' – a theme he was to take up relentlessly two years later.

A few weeks later a play, *Scene Three, Act One*, based upon *A Spaniard in the Works* and *In His Own Write*, directed by Victor Spinetti, was presented at the National Theatre. Sir Laurence Olivier expressed interest in the piece, but in the end it was just another one-minute Beatle event. It came, garnered a few headlines, and went, briefly feeding John's growing picture of

87

himself as the artistic all-rounder. Perhaps he was, but it was only into music that he was prepared to put his real energies. He had already decided that there were going to be no more books and no more sitting at a typewriter.

In November an EP of music from *Magical Mystery Tour* was released. It included John's 'I Am the Walrus', a further venture down the gobbledegook hallucinogenic road of 'Strawberry Fields Forever', and was a song made up of a series of odd lines scribbled down on pieces of paper during the previous eighteen months, with music based on the howling siren rhythm of a police car, and starting with the piercing accusation: 'I am he as you are he as you are me as we are all together, See how they run like pigs from a gun See how they fly, I'm crying.' It was the apotheosis of John's acid spell. Taken literally the lyrics didn't have any real meaning. But the collective effect of what was basically a two-tone incantation and litany of sinister creatures and distasteful and often ugly images was overwhelming. Once again John got himself into trouble. The BBC's new pop station, Radio One, discreetly advised its disc jockeys not to play the song. The lines 'Crabalocker fishwife, pornographic priestess, Boy you've been a naughty girl you let your knickers down' were considered unsuitable for broadcasting, despite the fact that no one, not even John, had any idea what they were about.

The cumulative effect of the images was indeed disturbing, but to John it would have been even more unsettling had he realized at the time that the reference to himself as the Walrus was not what he had intended. He had chosen the character from one of his favourite childhood stories, 'The Walrus and the Carpenter' in *Alice in Wonderland* by Lewis Carroll. He didn't realize that Carroll had intended the poem to be an allegory about capitalism and socialism. By identifying himself as the Walrus he had chosen the wrong hero. Just before his death he told *Playboy* exactly how he had come to write the song: 'The first line was written on one acid trip one weekend. The second line was written on another acid trip the next weekend ... Part of it was putting down Hare Krishna

... the reference to "Elementary penguin" is the elementary, naïve attitude of going around chanting Hare Krishna.' Whatever was intended, it came out as a musical *tour de force* of abstract poetry, and today it is among the rock classics, while 'Hello Goodbye', Paul's flippant hit single of the time, is virtually forgotten.

In Great Britain *Magical Mystery Tour* was shown in black and white at peak viewing time on BBC television on Boxing Day 1967. The reaction from critics and public alike was scathing. They simply could not comprehend it. For months people had been looking forward to a nice, jolly little Beatle show to make their Christmas complete. Instead they felt threatened and bewildered by what they saw.

Paul reacted quickest. The next morning he said: 'I suppose if you look at it from the point of good Boxing Day entertainment we goofed, really. Of course we could have got together a good screenwriter, a good director, and even some good songwriters, if you like, and asked them to produce a first-class Christmas show with the Beatles in it. That would have been the easiest thing in the world. But we wanted to do it ourselves . . . we wanted to present the viewers with something different from the phoney tinsel of Christmas shows.'

That evening Paul went on David Frost's television show and defended his work, charming away the critics. Time would tell how good the film was, he insisted. Time was to say that it wasn't at all a bad effort, and certainly nothing for the critics to be so viperish about. But the critics were not yet ready to see their family favourites step over into the avant garde.

From John there was silence. He let Paul take all the blame, although he confessed later that he had quite enjoyed it. It had been mainly Paul's baby, anyway. But by Christmas 1967 John Lennon had found a new interest in his life which was to become more important to him than any amount of fame, films, writing, art or even music. Her name was Yoko Ono, and for the next twelve years it was going to be difficult to think of the one without the other.

Yoko the Ocean Child

There are two schools of thought about Yoko Ono. To some people, mainly the friends John had before he met her, she is the woman who bewitched the most aggressive Beatle and turned him into her own, slightly lunatic, mirror image; who tantalized him away from his friends and co-Beatles and into her world of the avant-garde con. To others, mainly those who knew them both together, she was the sort of chum and companion that he needed. The truth is that Yoko did relentlessly pursue John at first, and that she *did* make him happy. Apart from his eighteen-month 'lost weekend' period between 1973 and 1975, they were together for nearly thirteen years, which is about as long as he was with the Beatles. And judging by the love songs to her on his last album, *Double Fantasy*, where she was given every alternate track to sing a love song to him, there is little doubt that he was as obsessed with her when he died as he had been a decade earlier when she was the most vilified woman in the world.

To many people Yoko Ono has always been a total enigma. John was always attracted to non-conformists, and there were few who conformed less than Yoko, or who proved to have such multi-faceted personalities. She was born under the sign of Aquarius (such things are important to Yoko) in 1933, the elder daughter of a governor in a Tokyo family bank and a mother who had always wanted to be a painter, but who really was something of a society hostess. Her family was rich and influential (her father spent most of the Second World War in Indo-Chino or Paris) and she was precociously bright. Her mother was Buddhist, her father Christian, and her school lessons were with a governess who took her in Bible reading and Buddhist scripture as well as calligraphy, music and Japanese culture.

'I was like a domesticated animal being fed on information,' she said later. 'They wanted me to be a pianist and my father would measure my hands to see if they were big enough. He had wanted to be a pianist himself and was disappointed to be a banker. I hated education, especially music, and I used to make myself faint to get out of it. They were very strict with me. I grew up to believe that God was always watching, and any mis-demeanours or bad thoughts had to be confessed to my mother. I never went so far as to read comics but I remember when I was about eight sneaking into my father's study to read adult books like Chekhov's *The Cherry Orchard*. Of course there was nothing improper in them, but my mother made me confess and it was a terrible ordeal. Then when I was older and received letters my mother always read them before I did. If one was from a man admirer she would blame it on some loose thoughts I had been having.'

When Yoko was eighteen her family moved to New York where her uncle represented Japan at the United Nations. As a child she had always written poems and plays, and when she enrolled at Sarah Lawrence College to study philosophy ('all the other girls thought of nothing but marrying Harvard graduates') she began her first book. It was called *Grapefruit*, and was a varied collection of abstract instructions such as :'Imagine the clouds dripping. Dig a hole in your garden to put them in . . .' or, 'Imagine letting a goldfish swim across the sky.' Many years later John would borrow the 'Imagine' concept for what he considered to be his finest song.

All this was, of course, in the early fifties (*Grapefruit* was not completed or published until 1964) while John would still have been at Quarry Bank High School in Liverpool. For years she tried, unsuccessfully, to be an artist in New York, but could find no one who would publish her work or put on her exhibitions. Then, when she was twenty-five, she met a Japanese musician,

Toshi Ichiyanagi, and married him. She was a virgin bride. They were different times, she said later.

The marriage in which Yoko had very much the upper hand lasted only a few, mainly unhappy years. She felt stifled by the establishment scene in which she was now moving and began to have affairs outside marriage. In the end she suggested to her young husband Toshi that he return to Japan. He did.

Shortly after that she decided that if no one was going to discover her as an artist she would have to discover herself. She rented a loft, converted it into a studio, and held happenings every other week. 'I was lying in bed one morning,' she recalled later when trying to describe what her happenings were like, 'and I was listening to the birds singing and felt that I wanted to put the sound into musical notes. But it was too complicated. So I thought if I can't do that perhaps it would be better to use the sound exactly as it was and wrote a one-note flute piece. The accompaniment was to be the sound of the birds singing. Then I gave out the instructions that the one note should be played in a forest while the birds were singing.'

At another concert (her description) she bought a baby-grand piano and played it with her body by rolling along the open strings. Yet another concert consisted of the boiling of a still of water and then listening until it evaporated. One of the men present was, she said, so excited that he filmed the whole event, only to discover later that he had forgotten to put any film in his camera.

Eventually, after John Cage, Peggy Guggenheim and Max Ernst had seen her happenings, she was given a one-woman show at a gallery on Madison Avenue in which people were invited to put a flame to a picture (usually a blank canvas) and watch the smoke. At last, the avant-garde coterie having begun to take notice, she gave concerts in Carnegie Hall and poetry readings on Canadian radio.

It is easy to poke fun at Yoko's avant-garde activities (John always said that *avant garde* was French for 'bullshit') but she must have truly believed in herself and in what she was doing to have kept hustling for so long. The concept of communication ruled her life, just as John was obsessed with the media. To Yoko it was not enough for an artist to present his work to the public. The public had to respond with a dialogue. Thus all her works were either unfinished or instructional.

In 1961 Yoko returned to Japan. In a fit of lonely depression after reading a damning review of her work, she attempted suicide and was sent to a mental hospital. While there her former husband brought a young American film-maker friend to visit her. His name was Tony Cox. There was a romance and as soon as she left the hospital she was married for a second time. The next year she had her first child, a daughter she called Kyoko, and the new family returned to New York.

Yoko later saw both her marriages as, in a sense, elopements. In this relationship, as before, she was the dominant partner. In 1966 Yoko moved to London for the Destruction of Art symposium at the Institute of Contemporary Art. Her husband and child followed and the family settled down in London.

The first fateful meeting between Yoko and John took place at an exhibition she gave at the Indica Gallery in Mason's Yard in London's West End, in November of that year. The Indica was one of a rash of new art galleries which erupted in prosperous London of the mid-sixties. John was invited to the preview and for some reason that he could never remember he decided to attend. In the middle of the gallery was a pair of step ladders. John climbed to the top. Attached to the ceiling was a canvas bearing a tiny word and a magnifying glass. John read the word. It was 'Yes'. He felt that was very positive. When he came down the steps he saw an instruction which said, 'Hammer a nail in.' He asked if he might, but Yoko replied 'No' as the exhibition was not due to open officially until the next day. At this point the gallery owner, John Dunbar, who was once married to singer Marianne Faithful, came over and suggested that Yoko allow John to hammer the nail since he was a millionaire and therefore a potential patron. Yoko replied that she would let John hammer the nail for five shillings.

John said: 'Well, okay, I'll give you an imaginary five shillings if you'll let me hammer in an imaginary nail.'

Yoko had found her soul mate. She said later: 'When John and I met I was living with my husband, Tony, but the first thing that crossed my mind was that I wouldn't mind having an affair with a man like that. It was so nice and pleasant and he seemed so sensitive and imaginative. I remembered every bit of our conversation afterwards, although I didn't realize that he was John Lennon. I was an underground person; and such an artistic snob. I knew about the Beatles, of course, but I'd heard about Elvis, and I wasn't interested in them.

'Then I met John again at another gallery opening for Claes Oldenbürg. This time I knew who John was and I was very uptight and afraid to go over and talk to him. He had on a kind of a scarf and was hiding most of his face and talking to someone. Then this nice-looking young man came over and began talking to me. It was Paul, but I didn't know. I thought maybe he was an art student or something. And he said, "My friend went to your exhibition and thought it was very good." So then John and I talked some more.'

In August of the next year, right in the middle of the silly season so far as the media was concerned, Yoko gained her very first popular notoriety in Britain when her film *Bottoms* was shown amidst much ribaldry from the popular press. Basically the film consisted of 365 close-ups of the bottoms of famous and unfamous people. It was good for the tabloids.

A few weeks later Yoko approached John again after John Cage, guru to the avant garde, came to London and, during the course of dinner, explained to her that he was compiling a book of twentieth-century music scores from Stravinsky to the Beatles.

'I thought maybe I could help,' said Yoko. 'So I called Robert Frazer and said I was trying to get in touch with the Beatles, but I was told they were recording and couldn't be disturbed. So then I called John at his home. Of course the number was unlisted, but I told the operator that it was very important and that yes, I knew him, and eventually she put me through and I explained to John what I wanted.'

John thought the best thing was for Yoko to go to the studios at Abbey Road and he'd show her some scores. But when she got there all he produced were a couple of pieces of paper with a few words scribbled on them. There were no scores. All the same the words were duly delivered to John Cage. John and Yoko never saw the book. It was lost in the post. John didn't care. He had only given Cage a few of the songs he didn't like, anyway.

Now firmly intrigued by Yoko, John agreed to finance her Half Wind Show at the underground Lisson Gallery. John had always been generous to the underground and at that time no one else thought there was anything more to his interest in Yoko than a passing whim. John didn't even go to the exhibition which was presented under the sub-title Yoko Plus Me, and consisted of ordinary household furnishings such as a bed, a chair, a pillow, a washbasin and a toothbrush, all sawn completely in half.

Yoko's next London happening was called Dance Event. By now she had begun sending John instructions through the post every day or so, cards which read 'Breathe' or 'Hit a Wall with your Head' or 'Keep laughing for a week'. John was bemused. Yoko was like no one he had ever met before. She gave him a copy of her book *Grapefruit* and he became increasingly attracted and yet exasperated by this strange, older, Oriental woman who insisted that her work was quite as important as his, and who insisted upon being treated as an equal. Yet still the friendship remained entirely platonic.

In February 1968 John and the other Beatles went off to the Maharishi's meditational institute at Rishikesh in the Himalayan foothills. For a time John toyed with the idea of taking Yoko with him, but in the end he didn't have the nerve to take her along as well as Cynthia. People would have thought it strange. Undeterred, Yoko continued to write him instructions during the month he stayed with the Maharishi.

'That was how it started,' explained Yoko. 'We didn't have any physical scene going, but mentally we knew that it had become a bit awkward for us both. I was going through a very bad time with my husband, so I went off to Paris for a while. The way I looked at it was that we were two adult people who were used to having affairs and all that. I thought that we'd both missed our chance to have an affair and would just remain friends . . . you know, how if you miss the moment then you can never go back to it. I was the aggressive one. I wrote letters to him in India saying things like "I'm a cloud. So when you look up and see a cloud you can think I'm there."' (Said John: 'These crazy letters kept coming driving me mad. But it was great, too.')

When he arrived home from India, John called Yoko and invited her down to his house. Cynthia had gone to Italy and Yoko's husband was in the South of France. 'I was wearing a purple dress,' said Yoko. 'John said later he thought that it was a good sign because purple is a very positive colour. We were very shy together at first. I mean he just couldn't say, "okay, let's make it." So he said we could either go upstairs to his studio and make some music, or stay downstairs and just chat.'

They went upstairs and played with John's recording equipment. The result was eventually released as *Two Virgins* album. 'It was very, very late at night when we finished. And then we just made love right there in the little studio.'

After that night John and Yoko were hardly seen apart again for nearly six years. John's marriage to Cynthia was over. The ballad of John and Yoko was just beginning. The days of the Beatles were already numbered.

For years after they first got together people would ask, 'What does he see in her?' Traditionally, when a famous star leaves his wife and family it is for some fantasy figure of femininity. But while Yoko was not unattractive, neither was she dazzlingly beautiful. She had a peaceful tranquillity in her expression, but she was no Candice Bergen, and when they first met she seemed uninterested in clothes other than a black sweater, black trousers and white gym shoes. But to John she was beautiful. She was a companion of the mind. They locked into each other's wavelengths instantly, and the more she was insulted the more John threw a chivalrous cloak of protection around her. During his marriage to Cynthia the slightly conservative Northern lower-middle-class man had emerged occasionally (as, for instance, when he refused to allow Cynthia to hire a nanny for Julian in 1967), but with Yoko that ambivalence of character – the good manners which Auntie Mimi had instilled into him coupled with the desire to shock and rebel – seemed to keep up a running dialogue. In many ways they were an old-fashioned romantic couple: in others they were druggy (heroin-sniffing at one point), freaky and outrageously publicity-conscious. Yet at all times they were a very good match for each other.

Probably to John the single most attractive feature about Yoko back in 1968 was that she was almost certainly the first woman John Lennon had met in the previous five years who was *not* a Beatle fan. She was aware of the hits, of course, but she had no idea who had written or who sung what. Even years later she would say without embarrassment: 'There are still some of John's works that I really don't recognize. Just as there are some of mine that he doesn't know.' She really didn't see the difference.

From Sexy Sadie
to the Two Virgins

Quite apart from his emotional turmoil over his new pen friend, John did not have the greatest of times meditating in Rishikesh. Ringo and Maureen lasted just ten days before deciding that they missed their children and sneaking back to London with funny stories of how the Maharishi's institute for meditation was really just like a Butlin's holiday camp.

'It wasn't what you'd call a hard life,' Ringo said. 'It was all quite luxurious actually. We'd sit about and meditate, eat in the canteen, go and bathe . . . just like a holiday really.'

For John, Paul and George it was a working holiday and, despite their rapid disillusionment with the Maharishi, they each wrote a prodigious number of new songs in the month they stayed.

'In the old days people would go off to Cornwall or to the desert or up into the mountains to write,' said John. 'I went to the Maharishi and I wrote some of my best songs there, regardless of what I was actually supposed to be doing in Rishikesh. I suppose in some ways it was a nice scene. It was secure and everyone was smiling. So I suppose the Maharishi was worth it – just for the songs. But the songs weren't happy. I was bloody meditating eight hours a day. But then when I wrote "Yer Blues" and said, "I'm so lonely, want to die", I wasn't kidding. That's how I felt.'

As so often when John recalled moments from his past, his attitude seemed contradictory.

In the summer and autumn of 1967 all four Beatles had told the world how the Maharishi had changed their lives, but by the spring of 1968 even George had lost his faith in the man – although he continues to live the mystic life to this day. The end of the affair for the Beatles and the giggling guru came eventually when it was alleged that the little holy man had made a pass at one of the lady film stars who had flocked out to join the four strangers in their Himalayan paradise.

'When George started thinking it might be true, I thought, well, it must be true,' said John.

The next day the whole Beatle force marched up to the Maharishi's bungalow and told him they were leaving. John was the spokesman for the group.

'Why are you leaving?' asked the Maharishi.

'If you're so cosmic you'll know why,' replied John, and left.

What really hurt was that suddenly they all felt very silly. They had thrown themselves whole-heartedly into the idea of the Maharishi and then had seen him for what he probably was – a rather cute, inoffensive operator playing upon the mystic susceptibilities of rich Western honkies.

'Maharishi,' sang John before he changed the name, 'what have you done, you made a fool of everyone, you made a fool of everyone, Maharishi, you'll get yours yet.'

But he never did.

The gap left in the lives of the four Beatles by Brian Epstein's death in 1967 led to a venture called Apple. Apple was like a tree with four roots. The idea was that it would act as an inspiration upon which all kinds of diverse talents would blossom and come to fruition. In practice Apple quickly became the meeting place for the spongers of the world, in the words of John. It was an idealistic venture, lacking proper organization, and before very long it left all four Beatles considerably the poorer, which was just another cause of acrimony when the break-up eventually happened.

Paul first explained the function of Apple like this: 'When we first started we were eighteen and wanted to get rich. And if there was a possibility of getting rich by singing we were willing to forget everything. Well, let's face it, that's what swinging London is all about, isn't it? But now we don't have to do things for ourselves any more. So instead of trying to amass money for the sake of it we are setting up a business concern at Apple – rather like a Western communism. We want to make it a complete business organization on the lines of ICI, not just for us but for the general good. Apple could be a social and cultural environment as well as a business environment . . . we've got all the money we need. So now we want to start directing the money into a business . . . something where the underwriters will get a decent share of the profits instead of just £2 a week, while we make a million.'

That was the theory. Apple was to become a new artistic centre for London. Money was available for films, publishing, fashion design, the electronic gimmicks of someone called 'Magic Alex' who came and went and worked no discernible magic at all, writers, new rock groups, underground newspapers, theatrical enterprises, artists . . . the list was endless, as were those who came with their begging bowls. A beautiful Queen Anne house was bought in London's Savile Row, completely renovated, re-decorated with white walls and green carpets, and the whole Beatle clan of Peter Brown, formerly Epstein's personal assistant, Neil Aspinall and Mal Evans – once roadies but now elevated to the status of managing directors and personal assistant – and Terry Doran – once 'a man in the motor trade' and now in charge of Apple Publishing – moved in. Everyone swam in the glamour of lavish Beatle generosity and learned how it felt 'to be one of the beautiful people'. On the third floor, former newspaperman Derek Taylor held open house for the world's press, and Scotch and Coke were consumed in abundance.

The benevolent John explained it in this way at the time: 'The aim of the company isn't a stack of gold teeth in the bank. We've done that bit. It's more of a trick to see if we can get artistic freedom within a business structure, to see if we can create things and sell them without charging three times our cost.'

If the Beatles ever believed in moderation they never showed it.

They were angels who rushed in where the biggest of fools would have feared to tread. But they were not simply foolish. There was a method in their madness. They had spent the past few years suffering nagging doubts that they were being ripped off by 'the men in the suits'. Now they were going to be ripped off again, by the freaks in the jeans.

For a while no one seemed to notice, especially not John who now threw himself whole-heartedly into the new lifestyle which Yoko presented for him. He had moved out of Kenwood, his home in Weybridge, and, while Cynthia began proceedings to end the marriage, set up home with Yoko in a flat owned by Ringo in London's Montague Square, using a room at Apple as their office. John himself began to take part in Yoko's conceptual art when in June he and Yoko went up to Coventry Cathedral to take part in an exhibition of British sculpture by planting two acorns in plant pots encircled by a wrought-iron garden seat. Unfortunately the next day the pots were moved to a different site. John was very cross. He said: 'The whole concept of our exhibit was one of growth and the fact that *we* planted it. Now that the acorns have been unplanted Yoko and I will have to go up to Coventry again to replant them. We took great care to plant the two acorns so that one faced east and the other faced west to symbolize that east and west have met through Yoko and me. We'll have to make sure that hasn't been spoiled. In fifty years' time people will understand what we're trying to say when there are a couple of lovely great oak trees up there rather than all those bits of old iron in funny shapes.'

At the time cynics shook their heads and laughed. Nutty John was into another of his phases. After LSD and the Maharishi he was now into planting acorns. People who had known the quick-witted, tough and cynical chief-Beatle of earlier days wondered whether too much acid had scorched his brain. John appeared not to care. In June he had his first exhibition at the Robert Frazer Gallery. He had caught the Yoko bug completely. The exhibition consisted of an assortment of boxes for various charities, a circular white canvas and 360 white balloons each of which bore the message 'You Are Here' and were released into the summer evening sky. The psychedelic, flower-power hero of exactly a year earlier had been replaced by the elegant artist in the Tommy Nutter white suit. The hair was growing longer and now being parted down the middle. John and Yoko were even beginning to look alike, and they had been together for less than three months.

Then at the end of July came the first of many John and Yoko stunts, although this one was done in the name of the Beatles. Nine months after the opening of the Apple boutique in London's Baker Street it was closed down, with instructions that all the clothes were to be given away free to customers. It was the idea of John and Yoko, and it made sense to the other Beatles, too. The previous autumn, when the shop was opened, Paul had said, 'Our idols used to be Elvis and Chuck Berry but now they are Marks and Spencer.' But it had never even begun to pay for itself and had become the first of many Apple millstones around their necks. In a single day at least £10,000 worth of goods (£30,000 by 1981 values), mainly clothes, were given away to astonished shoppers. By the afternoon the staff were simply standing in the street outside the shop giving away handfuls of shirts and frocks. It was a happening in the grand sixties' style. John and Yoko were delighted with it all, and began planning similar events, to take place as quickly as they could be arranged. Paul enjoyed it all, too. 'In future we're going to leave shopkeeping to Mr Tesco,' he said.

If the fans were worried by the transformation in the Walrus so, too, were the other Beatles. It was now time to begin recording again, but the once easy dialogue between John and Paul had ended with the arrival of Yoko. When Paul, Ringo and George assembled at the Abbey Road studios in the summer of 1968 they discovered that there were, in effect, now five Beatles. Earlier, whenever one of their assistants had begun to behave in a manner which they believed to be above his station the put-down had been instant and ruthlessly deflating: 'There are only four Beatles, you know,' they would say to the offending staff-member, and the caste system of their empire would be restored. But now, as they began to work on the songs which had been written in India, they found Yoko sitting on the speakers listening to everything, even occasionally making unrequested suggestions and even criticisms. None of the other girlfriends or wives had ever shown such temerity. When Yoko had first attended a recording session she had been surprised and disappointed at the constant rhythm with which most rock and roll is played, and John said later that for the first time he had felt ashamed of what he was doing. Now she was an integral part of John's life (recording or otherwise) and the other Beatles were angry and confused.

It is easy to see both points of view. To Paul, George and Ringo the four of them were the Beatles and they made the music. It had always been that way and it was difficult for them now to accept a gaze which they suspected of being critical watching over them. For John and Yoko it seemed the most perfect thing in the world. They wanted to be together night and day, and so they were. Yoko explained the feeling very well when she said that the three other Beatles behaved like in-laws towards her. One night she went to bed with a guy, she said, and the next night there were three in-laws standing over them.

The relationship between John and Paul was damaged forever. During the *Sergeant Pepper* sessions a year earlier they were still helping each other out on songs, and combining as with 'Day in the Life'. But from *The White Album* onwards it was every Beatle for himself. The comradeship of writing together and singing together vanished. The harmonies were things of the past. John and Paul each wrote and recorded his own songs, using the other members of the group merely as back-up musicians. Poor George couldn't even get John into the studios to record his songs, although Eric Clapton provided a more than adequate session musician, especially on 'While My Guitar Gently Weeps'.

Yet, surprisingly, from this brittle and tense four months of recording came some of the best Beatle recordings of all, and, as John said, 'some of the best songs I've ever recorded'.

His favourite from 1968, and quite the most poetic lyric he ever wrote, was 'Across the Universe'. He donated the first recording of this song to a World Wildlife Fund charity record, but he recorded it again for the *Let It Be* album. 'As a record it never really made it because I never recorded it right,' he said, 'but perhaps the lyrics will last.' The imagery is delicate – 'Words are flying out like endless rain into a paper cup' and 'Thoughts meander like a restless wind inside a letter box' – it was all so far from the 'Yellow matter custard dripping from the dead dog's eye' of the previous year. The gobbledegook of the acid period had been replaced by a self-conscious attempt at poetry.

The weeks in India were remembered everywhere on the record. In 'Dear Prudence' John wrote a gently affectionate song about Mia Farrow's sister who had also been in Rishikesh – 'the clouds will be a daisy chain, so let me see you smile again' – more enchanting images. His love of wordplay surfaced again on 'Glass Onion', in which he managed to work into the imagery the titles of five previous Beatle songs, as though he was mentally peeling away various layers and throwing out odd lines to please the people who looked for clues in his songs. 'The Walrus was Paul,' he sang, although it wasn't. 'I think I put that in because sub-consciously I was trying to be nice to Paul,' he said later, which may have been true. But it might also just have been a line which fitted and which amused his sense of perversity in this glance over the shoulder at recent Beatle history. In 'Cry Baby Cry' (a song partly written the previous year) we see again his admiration of Lewis Carroll in this inverted nursery rhyme – 'Twelve o'clock a meeting 'round the table for a seance in the dark, With voices out of nowhere put on 'specially by the children for a lark'. 'The Continuing Story of Bungalow Bill' was an allegorical attack on American involvement in Vietnam and 'the all American hero bullet headed Saxon mother's son'. The chorus line of 'Hey Bungalow Bill, what did you kill . . .?' may well have been partly inspired by the American anti-war chant of the time: 'LBJ, LBJ, How many kids did you kill today?'

In the song 'Julia', ostensibly about his mother, John mentioned

Yoko on record for the first time in the line 'Oceanchild calls me'. Yoko means Oceanchild in Japanese. Probably the most misinterpreted song of the sessions was 'Happiness is a Warm Gun' which, at the time, was seen by many as a song about heroin and the hypodermic syringe, but which was actually inspired by the cover of a gun magazine and an article of that title. The references to Mother Superior were about Yoko, while the lines about 'my finger on your trigger' was just a little bit of sex talk. John and Yoko spent nearly all their non working time in bed together in those days, they said, and that was before the bed-ins even started.

Altogether John had eleven songs on *The White Album,* Paul had twelve, George four and Ringo one. But the track which was to cause the most bickering between the Beatles was a John and Yoko aural freak-out called 'Revolution Number 9'. To most listeners it was a meaningless collection of sounds. When asked about the track, Paul, who actually hated it, would say diplomatically that he thought that sort of thing was all right in its own place – but that it's place was not on a Beatle album. This was one of the arguments which John won. At that time he complained often and vociferously that Paul was taking over Beatle albums, as he was certainly taking over writing the A sides for their singles, but the statistics don't support John's argument as much as he might have wished. On *Abbey Road* John wrote seven songs, Paul six and George two; while on *Let It Be* John wrote four, Paul five and George two. If John had real cause for complaint it may have been that more care was lavished on the production of Paul's songs than on his; but then Paul was going through a particularly productive spell with songs such as 'Hey Jude', 'Let It Be', 'The Long and Winding Road' and 'Get Back'. Part of the rivalry was caused by the fact that despite their differences the two Beatle writers plus George were going through the most creative spell of their lives, and there simply wasn't space for everyone's songs on their albums. Their individual talents were racing away with them, and there was no longer the good humoured jokiness to get them over their difficult spells together. John and Yoko were so bound up in each other that the three others felt like outsiders, while John and Yoko were aware of a burning animosity towards their relationship, and particularly towards her presence in the studio.

'It simply became very difficult for me to write with Yoko sitting there,' said Paul later. 'If I had to think of a line I started getting very nervous. I might want to say something like "I love you girl", but with Yoko watching I always felt I had to say something clever and avant garde. She would probably have loved the simple stuff, but I was scared. I'm not blaming her. I'm not blaming me. You can't blame John for falling in love with Yoko. John and I tried writing together a few more times, but I think we both decided it would be easier to work separately.'

Even before the marathon sessions for *The White Album* were completed the Beatles released their new single on their own Apple label. It was Paul's 'Hey Jude' backed with John's 'Revolution', and it quickly became the fastest selling Beatles single in years. John had to admit that 'Hey Jude' (which started life as Hey Jules when Paul was driving down to Surrey to see Cynthia and Julian after John had left) was good, but he was again peeved because his song was on the flip side. The melody to 'Revolution' was simple rock and roll, but the lyrics left no one in any doubt about John's political stance, and his attitudes about the student revolutionaries who took to the streets all over Europe in 1968. Whatever else John Lennon may have been into, he was certainly not into violence: and with a swingeing, questioning and cynical relish he turned on all those who looked to him for leadership in aggression; he wasn't going to be the Pied Piper of hate. 'When you want money for people with minds that hate, All I can tell you is brother you have to wait,' he sang, before turning his attention on the Chinese Cultural Revolution with 'But if you go carrying pictures of Chairman Mao, You ain't gonna make it anyone anyhow'. This wasn't only rock and roll. This was a put-down of the angry young men of the day, tied around the newspaper headline of the year, Revolution. It may not have been what they wanted to hear behind the *boulevard* barricades but it reflected the way John was thinking far more than his naïve slogan 'Power to the People' which he was to rush out in a moment of simplistic sloganeering a couple of years later.

In the meantime, away from the bickering of the recording studios, a wider controversy raged around the name of Lennon. Only a short time before he had been one of the lovable fluffy-haired mop-tops. Now he was rapidly becoming Public Enemy Number One as legions of the establishment queued up to attack him. In June the National Theatre production of the play, Scene Three, Act One, had been censored on the grounds of obscenity by order of the Lord Chamberlain's Office (which in those days was in charge of cutting out anything remotely sexual from theatrical productions), but then in October came the biggest anti-Beatles move of all after John and Yoko were charged with possessing marijuana.

For years a blind eye had been turned by the police to the Beatles' use of drugs. This apparent immunity from prosecution angered other rock stars such as the Rolling Stones who seemed to spend their entire lives in conflict with one police force or another. But when the immunity ended for John it did so with a vengeance. On the morning of 18 October a force of twelve police officers began hammering on the door to the flat in which John and Yoko were staying. They were, predictably, in bed at the time. When John opened the door he was confronted by a plain clothes detective sergeant from the Metropolitan Police Drugs Squad, who, bearing a search warrant, barged past him into the flat followed by two large dope-sniffing Alsatian police dogs.

'I was terrified,' said John. 'I thought the bloody Kray Brothers had come to get me. I didn't realize it was the police at first.'

The couple were hauled off down to the police station and charged with possession. The next day they appeared in court and were bailed. Outside the court they had to be protected by police from sightseers. But now there was a difference in the attitudes of both star and public. When John had had to run the public gauntlet previously, he had looked cocky and self-confident, while the fans had been eager, hysterical and admiring. Now suddenly John looked frail and vulnerable as he tried to protect Yoko from what seemed like a wave of hate bursting over them both. Beatle John was, with a little help from the press and police, destroying the public's image of him. And love was turning to hate.

The following month John pleaded guilty to the charge in Marylebone Magistrates Court and was duly fined £150, while in the House of Commons questions were asked about the necessity of employing twelve police officers on a simple drugs-bust. That might have been the end of the matter but for one thing. The United States Immigration Department were to use the conviction as a reason for hounding the Lennons for five years and it was not until 1975 that John was granted an immigrant's visa enabling him to travel freely in and out of the United States as he wished.

John always insisted that the dope had been planted on him and that he had only pleaded guilty to prevent Yoko, who was pregnant, having any further harassment and having to attend court. He told the BBC: 'I mean the thing was set up. The *Daily Mail* and the *Daily Express* were there, before the cops came. He'd called the press. In fact, Don Short had told us, "they're coming to get you", three weeks before. So, believe me, I'd cleaned the house out, because Jimi Hendrix had lived there before in this apartment, and I'm not stupid. I went through the whole damn house.' But even if the actual dope found had been planted, John could hardly claim innocence in the use and possession of drugs. For years he had been telling anyone who cared to listen that he smoked dope.

In November, while Cynthia was suing John for divorce, Yoko entered Queen Charlotte's Maternity Hospital. During her stay there, John slept at the foot of Yoko's bed. The day after the divorce became absolute Yoko had the first of several miscarriages.

The year of 1968 was almost over but John and Yoko had one more major controversy lined up for the now punch-drunk public. In December they released the famous *Two Virgins* recording made on the night they had first come together the previous April.

The record itself meant little to anyone other than the two lovers, but the cover meant a great deal. It showed them standing together quite naked, front and rear.

Viewed today, the cover of the record is merely an eccentric curiosity piece. But in those days, when the nudity in *Hair* was astonishing West End theatre critics, and long before *Oh! Calcutta!*, the world really did begin to think that John Lennon had become quite mad.

Yoko, never stuck for a word, had this to say: 'The album was actually John's idea. I know some people may think, "Ah, that bottoms girl Yoko has persuaded John into this," but I don't think my bottoms film inspired him. In fact I don't think he saw it. I know some men may think I have a bottom fetish, but when I made that film I was so embarrassed that I was never in the same room as the filming. I'm very shy. John is very shy, too. He heard one of the tapes of me singing and said that it should be an LP with a picture of me naked on the cover. I don't know why he said that. I suppose he just thought it would be effective. He didn't know me that well at the time. Anyway he sent me a drawing of me naked and I was terribly embarrassed. But when we decided to make the *Two Virgins* LP he decided that we should both be naked. He took the picture himself – with an automatic camera. It's nice. The picture isn't lewd or anything like that. Basically we are both very shy and square people. We'd be the first to be embarrassed if anyone were to invite us to a nude party.'

John viewed the public distaste with his usual honesty. 'The trouble is, I suppose, I've spoiled my image,' he said. 'People want me to stay in their own bag. They want me to be lovable. But I was never that. Even at school I was just "Lennon". Nobody ever thought of me as cuddly.'

Bagism, Shagism,
Dragism, Madism

Under their three-picture deal made in 1964 with United Artists the Beatles were committed to one more feature film, and no sooner was the *White Album* in the shops before preparations began to start filming *Let It Be*. While *A Hard Day's Night* and *Help!* had shown the zany four as lovable madcaps, *Let It Be* proved to be one of the most engrossing films about rock music ever made. The idea was simple: to film the Beatles making a new album. But because of the tensions which were now dividing the four musicians, director Michael Lindsay Hogg captured on film the rapidly dissolving partnership between Lennon and McCartney, the truculence of George when being criticized by Paul, and the cool philosophical attitude of Ringo who just kept drumming while the dream of the sixties fell to pieces around him. The film also showed how good the Beatles could be when they decided to jam together, first Paul picking up a song, to be joined by the others, but the easy-going jam sessions of earlier days were now submerged beneath the internecine personality battles. Throughout the sessions Yoko sat silently, her eyes rarely leaving the face of John. Certainly little joy was shown in *Let It Be*, although there was a lyrically romantic moment when John and Yoko waltzed around the Twickenham Film Studios to a playback of one of George's songs. When the film was released a year later it was said that Yoko appeared to be unhappy during the filming, to which John replied: 'Even the biggest Beatle fan couldn't have sat through the six weeks of misery which making that film was. It was the most miserable session on earth with the most miserable music going on and on and on, and everyone was expected to have a big smile going.'

He might have been right about the mood, but he was wrong about the music. That was very, very good, even by Beatle standards, and John did later admit that the film contained two of Paul's best-ever songs, 'The Long and Winding Road' and 'Let It Be'. Quite possibly John and Yoko were becoming increasingly paranoid about the animosity being shown to them by the press, public and the other three Beatles – who did not understand their activities any more than anybody else. Yoko felt that every time Paul sang 'Get back to where you once belonged' he looked directly at her. Paul said that he was not aware of doing this, but John and Yoko were so isolated in themselves, feeling that they were fighting a lone battle with the world, that virtually any look, glance or flippant remark could offend them. At this point a new element was added to the equation in the form of Linda Eastman, Paul's new girlfriend, who, with her daughter Heather, now accompanied Paul to the studios. While Jane Asher was the sort of girl to get on with her own career and leave Paul and John to sort out their differences, Linda brought her own little army in the shape of the Eastman family: her father Lee, an agent and music publisher in New York, and her brother John, a lawyer. John had found a new companion, abandoning Paul, at least in spirit. Paul had now found himself a ready-made family. No wonder the sessions were miserable.

The very last public Beatles performance was a bizarre event. The *Let It Be* film team set up their equipment on the roof of the Apple headquarters in Savile Row and the four Beatles performed their final session together for the cameras. The West End of London is hardly the place for an open-air pop concert and when the mega-watted Beatle amplifiers opened up one January afternoon irate businessmen immediately telephoned complaints to the police station a hundred yards away, while Regent Street shopgirls and Mayfair secretaries abandoned their posts and scurried around to Savile Row, peering heavenwards from whence the music was coming. Eventually a polite force of London bobbies climbed to the roof of the building, and the concert, all safely on film, was ended. That was 30 January 1969. It was the last time the Beatles were ever seen together.

In the meantime John was becoming increasingly concerned about the way money seemed to be flowing out of Apple, even quicker than the Beatles were able to earn it. In an interview with Ray Coleman in the music paper *Disc*, he said: 'It's been pie in the sky from the start. If it carries on like this all of us will be broke in six months. We haven't got half as much money as people think we have.' A few days later, while making another joke about 'being down to his last £50,000', he announced that American businessman Allen Klein had been appointed the Beatles' business adviser, despite opposition from Paul. The Beatles could hardly have made a more surprising choice, but John liked Klein at the time. Klein was the original backstreet orphan boy from New Jersey who had made it through the tough world of rock and roll because he was tougher than that world. He was manager of the Rolling Stones, having previously managed Bobby Darin and Connie Francis, but his open ambition was to manage the Beatles. When he read in a newspaper that John was worried about the way Apple had got out of control he flew to London and set up a meeting with John. 'Allen,' said John at the meeting, 'I just don't want to end up like Mickey Rooney.'

So Klein joined the Apple organization, first as adviser, and then as business manager (although Paul McCartney never recognized that) and some of the staff were sacked.

So the first part of 1969 went by. Copies of the *Two Virgins* were confiscated by American customs officials who considered the cover pornographic; John and Yoko made a film called *Rape*, which was shown on Austrian television, and was unique in that it was the only Lennon-Ono film so far not to be laughed at, and which did, in fact, win a measure of praise from critics other than the avant garde.

On 12 March 1969, Paul married Linda Eastman. None of the other Beatles were invited to the wedding. Three weeks later John and Yoko paid a similar non-compliment when, after holidaying in Paris, they suddenly flew by private jet to Gibraltar one morning and were married by a local magistrate. Peter Brown, the Beatles' personal assistant, was one of the witnesses. The bride wore a white mini-dress, a wide-brimmed white hat and white socks. John wore a white suit and carried a coat made out of human hair. The happy couple wore white tennis shoes. They chose Gibraltar because it was the easiest and quietest place they could find. Paul's marriage had been like an action replay of a Beatlemania carnival with thousands of girl fans mobbing the couple, even though Paul had tried to keep it secret.

Three hours after their wedding the Two Virgins were back in Paris, from where they moved to Amsterdam for their honeymoon – a week's bed-in for peace. Again the press took up their vicious cudgels, one revered columnist going so far as to imply that there was a base financial motive behind their antics. The savagery with which the Lennons were now attacked was almost frightening in its hate. Blithely newspaper pundits described Yoko as 'ugly'. 'I don't think she's ugly,' said John. 'I think she's beautiful.' No one could remember a time when a woman had had to stand such venomous attacks on her personal appearance. John was desperately hurt and angry. Nevertheless he and Yoko now decided that they would send an acorn to every world leader in the name of peace. It was a slightly less silly idea than their stunt of a few months earlier when they had appeared at the Albert Hall in a large bag. To most people everything from bagism to bedism to acornism was silly. But it was harmless. The acorns did not achieve world peace, but then neither did the Vietnam peace talks in Paris where diplomats spent weeks arguing about the shape of the table. To the Lennons it was important: to most people it was silly. But at the very worst it was only irrelevant.

Many people still find it difficult to see exactly what John was hoping to achieve with his honeymoon bed-in. His logic was that he was very famous and that people would write about him whatever he did. So why not stay in bed, invite the world's press and then tell them that they must write about the concept of peace? He was right in that he achieved saturation publicity; but it was mainly very dismissive. When he was criticized for not doing more for peace by donating funds to charity, he would reply that he did that as well. He sincerely thought that by staying in bed at the Amsterdam Hilton and talking in marathon sessions he could affect the lives and minds of the young people who looked to him for leadership. Of course he also saw the funny side of it. He was still the joker. He explained this by saying he would rather see his own picture in the front pages of the newspapers and know that he was making people laugh, than the faces of politicians, for whom he had always had scant respect. He didn't mind playing the clown if he thought it might have some worthwhile results.

Bagism was more difficult to understand. The first bagism event happened at an underground Christmas party at the Royal Albert Hall at Christmas, 1968, when John and Yoko appeared tied up in a large white bag. This was more of a Yoko-inspired event, the idea being taken from the theme of Saint-Exupery's *The Little Prince*: 'the essential is invisible to the eye.' By making themselves anonymous in this bizarre way, the force of what they were saying would not be misinterpreted by physical appearance, they argued. It was not a theme the Lennons were to pursue to any extent.

Most people would have gone away and hidden their heads from the public gaze in the spring of 1969, so bad was the feeling in Britain towards John and Yoko, but the more they were attacked, the more they retaliated by increasing their stunts. They formed their own company, Bag Productions, to make their own films, one of which, *Self Portrait*, was a fifteen-minute slow-motion piece showing John's penis in erection.

There were more records, too, more albums which, to most people, sounded like collections of unrecognizable sounds, such as

The Wedding Album and *Life with the Lions* – a sort of follow-up to
the *Two Virgins* – which included the heartbeat of the baby Yoko
had lost the previous November. It all seemed self-indulgent and
narcissistic, but John had lost little of the wit. Now he made jokes
against himself and Yoko. When she said that she had grown to
like rock music, he scoffed: 'Yes, at first she was afraid to sing with
a band, but now we only have to play four bars and she's off
wailing . . . aaaaaagghh. Take her anywhere and she does her
number.' To which Yoko replied: 'When I was young I wanted
to be a great opera singer . . . and appear at somewhere like La
Scala.'

'You also wanted to sing in a night club, didn't you?' said John
derisively. He still had the happy knack of putting someone down,
even Yoko, when he thought they were being pretentious. They
were just happenings. You were expected to take them or leave
them, but since he and Yoko had enormous egos he expected
people to take them rather than leave them.

The volume of newspaper space criticizing them amused him.
He said: 'Newspapers have spent ten times as much space
knocking what we are doing than they have writing about the
events. I get clippings from all over the world about things I've
never done and places I've never seen. I often wonder what the
hell's going on. There's some guy in New York saying he has my
hair coat, and it's over there in that cupboard. I've never actually
worn it. It carries on by itself.'

'And I'm the bitch,' said Yoko.

'That's right. When Yoko met me she was suddenly turned into
the Seven Dwarfs.'

'I also wanted to win a Nobel Prize and be the first female Prime
Minister of Japan,' said Yoko.

'And I wanted to write *Alice in Wonderland* and be bigger than
Elvis,' said John. 'I like being rich and famous, but I sometimes
think it would be nicer to be rich and famous and invisible, to get
all the credit and the fun, but to be invisible when I went out so that
no one recognized me.'

'We could go to Japan and maybe we wouldn't be recognized,' said Yoko. 'All foreigners look alike there.'

'Bullshit,' said John.

He knew how famous he was. At that time he wouldn't have had it any other way. While a small part of him may have resented the intrusion of the press into his life, another part could not help but be a maddening self-publicist. No sooner had the Beatles' new record 'Get Back' hit the top of the charts than John had telephoned Paul, booked time at the studios and they were recording 'The Ballad of John and Yoko', as a duo, since neither Ringo nor George was available. Paul played bass and drums, while John did all the guitar work. It was a momentary reconciliation of the super-Beatles but it was to be a one-day affair. The song, released in May 1969, was one of the Beatles' weakest singles, but it showed the new direction in which John was now working. It was an 'instant' record, no sooner recorded than released, and was totally personal to the Lennons. Of course, even a new single by a Beatle could not pass without controversy, and this time the row came over the line 'Christ you know it ain't easy . . . the way things are going, they're going to crucify me.' It opened all the old wounds of 1966 and his 'Beatles are bigger than Jesus' line, and again got him charged with being blasphemous in America where many stations banned the record. The old element of self-mockery had survived the hate intact, however. 'Made a lightning trip to Vienna, eating chocolate cake in a bag. The newspapers said "she's gone to his head", They look just like two gurus in drag.' In style it was basic rock and roll ('Johnny B. Paperback Writer', said John), with Paul's bass line being taken directly from the Elvis hit of 1956, 'Don't Be Cruel'. It was also the very last time Paul was to sing harmony alongside John on the chorus. Musically, it was a throwback to the Cavern days, including a few guitar phrases from 'The Honeymoon Song', an old Cavern favourite, and it was in a style that John was to work with repeatedly over the next few years.

Meanwhile there was more goading of the press. In April, John

Winston Lennon officially changed his name to John Ono Lennon in a ceremony on the Apple roof, and then in May the Lennons flew to Montreal for a ten-day bed-in. He would have preferred it to have taken place in the United States, but since his conviction for possessing cannabis the previous November he had been unable to obtain a visa to enter the USA. It was during this 'event for peace', as it was described, that the song 'Give Peace a Chance' was written and recorded, with the help of an eight-track mobile recorder, plus Timothy Leary, Tommy Smothers and Beatles' press officer Derek Taylor. The song was typical of John. Just when he was being universally derided for his silliness he knocked off a song which would become a world anthem for peace movements, and, in variation, a mass chant for soccer supporters. It was a song which because of its timing became an anti-Vietnam war hymn for peace over the next few years, although it was hardly more than a much-repeated eight-bar chorus: 'All we are saying is give peace a chance.' The concept of the Plastic Ono Band had been born, and at the end of July the song was released as a single, John's first without the other Beatles.

Allen Klein was not having an easy time as manager of the Beatles. In March music publisher Dick James had sold his entire holding in Northern Songs to ATV, the television and entertainments group run by Lew Grade. John and Paul, the two writers whose work had provided more than seventy per cent of the income for the company over the past five years, felt as though they had been stabbed in the back by the moneymen. 'Uncle' Dick had been with them since 1963, and now he was apparently taking his profit and leaving. This only made John more resentful of everyone who appeared to be trying to take advantage of him, and he wanted Klein to wrest control of the songs from ATV. Klein failed to do this. To compensate for his failure, Klein renegotiated a new contract with EMI in Britain and its Capitol subsidiary in America, which was to make both them and himself (his salary was said to be twenty per cent of the Beatles' total income) considerably richer.

That the Beatles were able to work creatively at all during this period is enormously to their credit. While Paul's father-in-law, Lee Eastman, squabbled with Klein for control of the Beatles' affairs, and while they watched themselves and all their songs being sold to some impersonal corporation, they continued to write and record. 'You never give me your money, you only give me your funny papers and in the middle of negotiations you break down,' sang Paul, as he looked around him at the jungle of businessmen who were fighting for the hearts of the most popular people in the world.

During the summer of 1969 the Beatles' last album, *Abbey Road*, was recorded at the studios of that name. To say that the Beatles recorded together is wrong: they rarely worked in groups of more than two. Producer George Martin patiently sat through the rows of all the recording. This time it was George who was fed up, mainly because he felt, justifiably at this point, that he had not had enough say in the Beatles' recordings, and he was aggrieved that with two exceptions he had never been given even the flip sides of Beatles' singles, which is a very lucrative business for the songwriter. Eventually he came back and somehow the album was finished. It was by no means the Beatles' best work, although it contained George's hit, 'Something'. John's contributions were varied. There were two snatches of songs which he had never bothered to finish, both written years earlier: 'Mean Mr Mustard' and 'Polythene Pam'.

'They were both hits I'd written in India which I found and which weren't worth finding,' he said. 'On "Polythene Pam" I used a strong Liverpool accent because she was supposed to be a mythical Liverpool scrubber, like a whore, dressed up to kill in her jackboots and kilt.'

As a way of finishing the album Paul worked both pieces into a fifteen-minute section which contained half a dozen other bits and pieces, and tried to make a virtue out of necessity.

Of John's other tracks, 'Come Together' was one of his favourites: 'Timothy Leary's wife wants it as a campaign song for them,' he said, without specifying which particular campaign she wanted it for, while 'I Want You' was a song about Yoko. 'There was nothing else I could say about her. She's just a heavy, funky lady. That guy on *Tonight* with the peg leg and haircut [the late Kenneth Allsop] made some snide comments about the lyrics, but she's just a heavy funky lady, like it says.'

The album had the expected success, but even before it was released John had decided that it was time for him to leave the Beatles.

In the middle of September he accepted, on a whim, an invitation to play at a rock and roll revival concert in Toronto. Gathering around himself a group of musicians which included Eric Clapton on lead guitar, Klaus Voorman on bass and drummer Allen White, he flew to Toronto and appeared as a surprise guest before 20,000 fans along with his old idols Chuck Berry, Gene Vincent, Jerry Lee Lewis and Bo Diddley. Before the show he was so nervous that he threw up several times, but after it he was jubilant. He said: 'I don't care who I have to play with but I'm going back to playing rock on stage. I can't remember when I had such a good time. Yoko, who you can say was playing bag, was holding a piece of paper with the words to the songs in front of me. But then she suddenly disappeared into her bag in the middle of the performance and I had to make them up because it's so long since I sang them that I've forgotten most of them. It didn't seem to matter. Then she did her wailing bit. It was great.'

John called the impromptu group the Plastic Ono Band, and a recording of the performance was later released as an album entitled *Live Peace in Toronto*.

So far during 1969 hardly a day had gone by without the name of John Lennon appearing in a newspaper headline because of some controversy or business disagreement. But on 25 November he was to outshine even his own ability to shock. Quite simply, he decided to return his MBE to the Queen in protest, he said, at the

British involvement in the war in Nigeria, Britain's support of the Americans in Vietnam and because his new record 'Cold Turkey' was slipping down the charts. It was another publicity stunt, but this time he had offended the very fibre of the British establishment. The reference to 'Cold Turkey', his second Plastic Ono single, was a flippant silliness which was probably an error of judgment. When asked to explain, he said that he wanted to begin the seventies as simply John Lennon, not John Lennon MBE. The person who suffered the most indignity was the long-suffering Auntie Mimi, who had proudly displayed the medal on her television set ever since John had been given it in 1965. 'Here, Mimi, you deserve it more than I do,' he had said, handing it over to her four years earlier.

Now it was of more value to him as a form of protest. If accepting it had been a mistake, and he thought it had been, sending it back was a bigger one. It was an empty gesture: he was now well past the point of media overkill, but he was hooked on headlines. He couldn't get enough of them. The lazy, indolent but witty Beatle had become a frenzy of energy. He picked up and dropped causes in a roller-coaster of activity, without even attempting to investigate whether the causes were always worthy of the attention he was trying to draw to them. He became, in his own words, 'a crutch or a sponge for the world's lepers'. The parents of James Hanratty, who had been hanged six years previously for a murder, sought his support in publicizing their request for a Queen's Pardon for their dead son and he helped; he campaigned on behalf of American Indians; and he gave funds to help form a commune known as The Black House in London's Camden Town. He was always well intentioned, but his energies were so dissipated as to be often virtually meaningless, and in the case of The Black House and its leader, Michael X, he was supporting a man of very dubious motives. In a sense this naïveté was touching, but it was also infuriating for those around him, who sensed that he was being taken in.

By the end of 1969 many of those who were not around him, and

29. John Lennon's eight-year musical apprenticeship must have seemed interminable. The day a school friend played him 'Heartbreak Hotel' he knew what he wanted to be. Within a few months he had his own group – The Quarrymen. This is the earliest known picture of them. Paul was to join shortly afterwards.

30. It was playing marathon sessions in Hamburg and then in The Cavern that the musical style of the Beatles was formed and polished.

31. *Above:* by the time the Beatles last appeared at The Cavern in 1963 they were already household names in Britain. *Below:* before the end of the year they were to play at the London Palladium in the Royal Variety Performance before the Queen Mother.

32. 'I'm a competent guitarist,' John would say. 'I can make it move.'
Above: an early recording session (1963). *Below:* on tour in Paris (1965).

33. 'To be a Beatle you had to completely humiliate yourself,' he said later;
but during the mid-sixties he was rarely seen without a grin and a joke. Here he
is at a television studio in 1966.

34. 'How often did we enjoy a show? Once in how many weeks of touring . . . all that talk about gigs and clubs is a dream. It was more like a nightmare,' he said in 1970. *Above:* the Beatles at Munich in 1966. *Below:* appearing before 60,000 hysterical fans at Shea Stadium in New York (1966).

35. The Sergeant Pepper album in the Indian summer of 1967 was to become a landmark in the history of rock from which everyone interested in popular music would henceforth chart his career.

36. Yoko Ono's first public appearance on a rock and roll stage alongside John at London's Lyceum ballroom in December 1969.

37. 'We've built a cottage industry,' said John in 1971 when he had a recording studio put into his home at Ascot to record the *Imagine* album. A few months later he left the house and went to live in New York.

38. John's last appearance on stage was as a guest with Elton John at Madison Square Gardens in November 1974 when they sang 'Whatever Gets You through The Night', 'Lucy in the Sky with Diamonds' and 'I Saw Her Standing There'.

39. In August 1980 John Lennon returned to the Hit Factory recording studios in New York to make his first album in five years. 'It's my time again,' he said.

not witnesses to the quips and jokes and self-mockery, were becoming convinced that John Lennon was indeed insane. Those who were involved with his day-to-day events, fads and obsessions saw him in quite a different light.

'Henry Ford knew how to sell cars by advertising,' he would say. 'I'm selling peace at whatever the cost. Yoko and I are just one big advertising campaign.'

The difference was, of course, that Henry Ford could tell how successful his campaign was by the number of cars sold. There was no possible way of quantifying the success of the Lennons' campaign. But because John was also Beatle John, he was surrounded by a lot of back-slapping 'yes-men'. In those days John and Yoko had no particularly close friends, and since he hardly spoke to Paul any more there was now no one, apart from the newspapers, to debunk his wilder extravagancies. And, although he was the complete media man, he tended to be selective in what he believed in the newspapers. His fame as the leader of the Beatles gave him access to all kinds of avenues, and he was never backward in using them. To have been a Beatle in 1965 was, one of them once said, like being the calm at the centre of the hurricane. Everything happened around them. Now John, aided by Yoko, had for a short time become the hurricane itself.

Years later, reflecting upon his peace mission and the endless gimmicks, he was to say: 'I know that some of what we have done together looks silly. But I don't regret any of it. Why should I? We did it, after all. And I know that a lot of what we say is repetitious and ordinary. But what we have to say is really very simple. We are not ashamed of its simplicity. We are just determined to go on saying it until someone does something about it. *You* try and do ten million interviews a day and try and think of something different to say each time . . .'

The Clown Prince
of Peace?

The 'man of peace' image which John Lennon began to adopt in 1969 may have been publicly ridiculed in Great Britain, but in America he found a rich vein of sympathy among many young and some older people who were appalled and frightened by the war in Vietnam. In Britain the war was something which had been fought more than twenty years earlier, while the campus revolts of 1968 had been largely a European and American phenomenon. John and Yoko may have found themselves quite out of step at home, but not so in America. Bearing this in mind, he and Yoko flew to Toronto (the nearest place John could get to the USA) just before the Christmas of 1969 for a weekend's frantic activity, which included a television show hosted by the late Marshall McLuhan, and a meeting with the Canadian Prime Minister, Pierre Trudeau. In between engagements John made dozens of calls to radio stations, had meetings with Dick Gregory and Marshall McLuhan, and even managed to sign five thousand copies of his famous 'erotic' lithographs.

When the Lennons later left England to live permanently in New York it was easy to understand their reasoning. In the United States and Canada they were taken seriously, rather like whimsical messiahs. In Britain John would forever be nutty John, the Beatle who became unhinged. In 1969 English fans treated Paul as Prince Charming, but they were afraid and disturbed by John. He described himself as the Clown Prince of Peace, but his principality lay only in the New World. There, quiet student fans on seeing the

Lennons' huge black limousine would smile and make the peace sign. There was no hysterical mobbing. But there were serious, flattering and academic leaders in the newspapers.

It had been arranged that John and Yoko would stay at the home of veteran rock and roll star Ronnie Hawkins and his wife Wanda at their house at Streetsville, a few miles from Toronto. The weekend had been arranged mainly by Ritchie Yorke, an Australian journalist and hustler living in Canada, with the help of Anthony Fawcett, then the Lennons' English personal assistant who was also a self-proclaimed art critic, and another likeable hustler. The only thing John really knew about his host before descending upon him with his entourage was that Hawkins had had a couple of hits in the fifties, and that 'he used to sort of waggle his arse' when he sang.

The weekend came as something of a surprise to Wanda Hawkins. She had been preparing to celebrate an ordinary family Christmas with an ordinary family-sized Christmas tree when suddenly her husband told her that they would be expecting a few extra guests. They can hardly have had any idea of what they were letting themselves in for. Within hours a man who represented Capitol Records in Canada appeared in a huge Chrysler at their ten-acre smallholding and unloaded the biggest white, synthetic, gingham-draped Christmas tree anyone had ever seen, together with a gilded cage bearing two pure white, live, but uncooing doves. An hour or so later the men from the telephone company came and installed six new lines. Then, before the day was out, a macrobiotic cook together with his Zen cookbook was hired, plus a girl with a lot of gold teeth who was chauffeured out to Streetsville daily just to do the washing up.

Then there they were, the Lennons, Ritchie Yorke, Fawcett, the man from Paris with his five thousand lithographs, a couple of Canadian rock promoters who were bent upon getting John to agree to a concert in Toronto the following summer (in aid of peace, of course) and a varying number of wives, girlfriends, and hangers-on and flotsam and jetsom of Toronto rock society. And then came the news teams, television producers, sound men, cameramen and interviewers, radio interviewers and, of course, journalists . . . and every one of them seemed to have wives, girl-friends and children.

Within a couple of hours all of Wanda Hawkins's pre-Christmas polishing and cleaning had been ruined as dozens of strange people tramped in from the eight inches of snow, and wandered around her house; while her children sat quietly, as they had been told, and wondered why there were huge signs everywhere saying 'Britain Murdered Hanratty', or lost themselves under the thousands of 'War Is Over' signs.

The Hawkins family were excellent hosts. Everyone was made welcome, and they even gave up their own bedroom to John and Yoko. Wanda slept with the children in one room, Anthony Fawcett shared with a journalist in one of the other children's bedrooms, and presumably big Ronnie, a huge bear of a bearded man who laughed throughout everything, must have found somewhere to sleep. 'This is the greatest thing that could possibly happen to me,' said Ronnie. He had just made his first rock and roll album for years and was suddenly receiving megatons of publicity by association. 'I've suddenly found that I've got a whole lot of friends I haven't seen for years,' he said, sardonically.

Everything the Lennons did in Toronto that weekend provoked exaggerated compliments. In London, although they were continually berated by the press they could behave more or less like normal people, since most of those working for them had been around for years. But in Canada, and later in America, their very presence summoned smiles, interest and flattery. One day, in a free moment between speaking to the press and television, Yoko went shopping and returned with a pink trouser suit. The reaction of the women in the household (Wanda Hawkins, who was brushing snow out of the hall, excepted) was hysterical in its approval. The outfit was at once 'pretty', 'chic', 'beautiful', 'smart but casual' . . . every compliment which came to hand was thrown at it.

Yoko didn't even acknowledge their attentions. 'Do you like it, John?' she asked.

'Yeah, it's great,' said John, looking up from a copy of the London *Daily Mirror* in which a full-page article had been given to describing him as Clown of the Year.

'That's all right then.'

When the Lennons weren't out being interviewed they were either skidooing on the snow, along with the ever-grinning retinue, or signing the lithographs, a series of erotic pictures showing John and Yoko in various positions of love-making, and which John said he had 'knocked off one afternoon' at the request of someone from Consolidated Fine Arts. Why, he was asked, do you draw so many pictures of the act of cunnilingus? He grinned naughtily. 'Because I like it,' he said.

John was shy about his art at this time. He had no idea whether or not he was any good and felt that he would not be considered seriously anyway. Yoko had no doubts: 'Better than Picasso,' she said.

Since the lithographs were on expensive paper and later to be sold at great profit (£150,000), a human chain of everyone in the house, excepting Yoko, was made to hand the lithographs to John and then stack them in neat piles on the far side of the living-room. John was signing at the rate of sixteen a minute. 'It was easier during Beatlemania,' he said at one point. 'Mal and Neil [Mal Evans and Neil Aspinall] used to sign for us. It was Neil who signed the pictures which were sent to Prince Charles.'

Other lithographs showed Yoko masturbating and after being shown in a Bond Street gallery in London the collection was referred to the Director of Public Prosecutions. The lithographs reflected the mutual obsession which John and Yoko had at this time. In the mid-sixties John had told journalist Maureen Cleave, 'I hope I grow out of being so sex mad. Sex is the only exercise I ever get.' And when she pressed him on the point of marital fidelity he had replied: 'Do you mean to say that I might be missing something?' The question of marital infidelity never appeared to

125

cross his mind during the first few years that John and Yoko were together, and their relationship had a very strong physical element to it. He said: 'We're not immune to sex, you know. We're always sussing each other out. But you have to weigh up whether or not it's worth it. There's a difference between fancying other people and having sexual fantasies about them. We wouldn't mind going to see a bit of a sex show, you know, being voyeurs, but we wouldn't want to join in.'

'We know the odds too much,' said Yoko. 'Before we met we were both too free. I always felt I was the creative one in the family and so I had to have my freedom. Now John and I have made a match. We don't really have close friends because when you do get close to another couple you start thinking in terms of a communal scene, not necessarily of sex, but of sharing everybody. So we try to keep a slight distance from everybody, even with our own children. We know that if we start to love our children too much then it will draw us slightly further apart. It's terrible, but even with them we keep a little distance . . . Sometimes I think that because Julian is with Cynthia, and Kyoko is with her father that we have the best two baby-sitters in the world looking after our children.'

John listened to all this and then added: 'Our main trouble is finding people who are like us, who get the same kicks as us.'

'And we are both very jealous people,' said Yoko.

'I'm jealous of the mirror,' said John.

'We're also haunted by our past,' said Yoko. 'When we first got together we told each other about everything and for a long time it was just torture thinking about it.'

One afternoon during that weekend in Canada the owner of a New York gallery flew up to Toronto to discuss an exhibition of John's lithographs in New York. 'Your debut as an artist in New York will undoubtedly be the most exciting event for years,' he said to John, completely straight-faced. 'You are really the prince of peace. In fact we're going to appeal that you get the Nobel Peace Prize.'

The assembled company thought that was a wonderful idea,

and quickly fell to debating whether or not John should accept the
prize were it to be offered. John just laughed his way through it all.
He was used to bullshit. That was all he ever got from strangers.
People either loved him or they hated him. This was a welcome
respite after eighteen months of being pilloried in England. Then
almost as suddenly as the peace prize had been brought up it was
dropped, and the conversation returned to the New York
exhibition which was to include a masquerade party of couples
dressing up as John and Yoko. John thought this was funny, too,
and suggested to Yoko that he might be able to get off with one of
the other Yokos. Then he had second thoughts: 'No, that wouldn't
work, you'd be able to have your choice of all the other Johns,' he
said. Everyone laughed very loudly and thought that very funny.
Then Yoko said: 'I'll go and change.' To which John added: 'Oh
good, I'll come and watch,' and together they left the room,
leaving the company to lunch on the Lennons' macrobiotic
cookies, macrobiotic bread, brown rice and seaweed, which
everyone praised hugely.

There is something peculiarly debasing in seeing people
buttering up to a star so wantonly. To John it had become a way of
life. He might have imagined that he could always spot the joker in
the pack, but he was frequently quite wrong in his judgment of
people. He would not suffer fools gladly, but on many occasions
the greater the charlatan the higher John's regard for him.
Sometimes it seemed that John's pack of cards was just about full
of jokers. 'Don't you think the joker laughs at you,' he had sung in
'I Am the Walrus'. But often it laughed at him.

On another afternoon comedian Dick Gregory came up to
Toronto. He was just as effusive in his praise as the art dealer. But
he was also funny. He understood completely the media blitz that
the Lennons had been building up. His idea of an event would even
have out-Yokoed Yoko.

'I reckon the best way of making people aware of poverty is to
eat two people,' he said. 'You could tell the media before so that

there would be reporters and television people there to cover the event. They wouldn't let on because they'd be frightened that the police would come and stop the people being eaten and spoil their story. It would soon get to the state where the fat cats would be afraid to go out on to the streets because they would figure they'd be the first choice for eating.'

The fact that John had never actually read a word of what Marshall McLuhan had written ('I haven't read a book in ten years. I know what he stands for') did not appear to worry him when he took part in a live chat show on nationwide Canadian television. 'How you doin', Marshall McLuhan,' he said, and proceeded to explain why Toronto was suddenly being saturated with huge War Is Over signs, the cost of which he was bearing from his own pocket, like all of his ventures. If he got hard up he could always go and write a few songs, he said.

During the course of the interview McLuhan asked a question about dope, and John immediately seized upon the chance to preach to the young. 'Speed kills,' he said simply. It was probably the first time he had condemned any drug openly.

John's attitude towards dope never stopped changing. Always a man to want to experience everything at first hand, he ran through a vast array of drugs during the course of his life, even going so far as to begin sniffing heroin at one point in the late sixties and early seventies. His record 'Cold Turkey' was banned in many places, but it was an anti-drug song about the miseries of coming off drugs and the pain involved.

Later in the programme McLuhan asked the expected question about the Beatles. John grinned: 'The Beatles are like an ancient monument. They ought either to be changed or scrapped.'

For once in his life he was actually avoiding giving a straight answer. He had already told the other Beatles and Allen Klein that he had left the group. In the privacy of his bedroom later that night he said: 'Allen's persuaded me to keep it quiet until the *Let It Be* album comes out. Then I'll make an announcement.'

A few days before Christmas the Lennons had a fifty-minute

meeting with Pierre Trudeau. For a man who only five weeks earlier had supposedly insulted the Queen by sending back his MBE, this was a considerable personal coup. The Prime Minister treated him with the greatest respect. For once John Lennon was impressed with someone in the establishment. And when he arrived back in England he was flattered by the prestigious BBC programme *Tonight* by being named Man of the Decade. His message was getting through.

Inevitably there were a couple of sour postscripts to the Toronto weekend. The rock and roll peace festival never happened, and six months later Wanda Hawkins was still trying to get the stains out of her carpets, while Ronnie Hawkins was wondering who was going to pay the two-thousand-dollar telephone bills which had been run up over the weekend. John was never mean, in fact he could be generous to a fault, but by the time he heard about the unpaid bills his public peace junket was over and he had retreated into his reclusive shell.

In the end it was Paul who took the initial blame for breaking up the Beatles, which was ironic since he was the one who had tried hardest to keep the group together after Brian Epstein died.

The final rows had been in the autumn of 1969 when John and Paul fell out over a press party for the *Abbey Road* album. Paul wanted to invite about twenty journalist friends. John wanted the underground press to come as well. In the end there was no party at all. Nor was John happy about some of the tracks on the album. He hated 'Maxwell's Silver Hammer' and a song called 'Teddy Boy', which Paul eventually put on to his own first solo album.

In the end Paul had suggested that the only way they were ever going to get back to playing together again was by going out and playing as a band. 'I didn't want us to go out and play to 200,000 people so I hit upon the idea of playing surprise one-night stands in unlikely places – just letting a hundred people into the village hall and then locking the doors. So one day we had a meeting and I told the other Beatles of my idea and asked them what they thought.

John said, "I think you're daft. I'm leaving the Beatles. I want a divorce."'

For nearly six months while John was off making records with the Plastic Ono Band, Paul wondered what to do. In the end he put a recording machine into his home and produced his first solo album, *McCartney*. A few days before its release he telephoned John and told him that he had a new album due out a couple of weeks before the Beatles *Let It Be* album, and that he, too, was leaving the Beatles. He didn't quite say it so directly but a hint in a press statement was enough, and the world's newspapers ran the headline: 'Paul Quits the Beatles'.

John was furious. He had been the one who had started the Beatles; he felt it was his job to finish them. He was angry with himself for staying silent for so long, and angry with Paul for apparently using the veiled announcement to help sell his new album. The acrimony was intense. Paul was furious that Phil Spector had been called in to remix the *Let It Be* album and had added a female choir to 'The Long and Winding Road' without asking for his opinion. It was Paul, however, who summed up the real reason for the Beatles' break up when he said: 'John's in love with Yoko and he's no longer in love with the other three of us. And let's face it, *we* were in love with the Beatles just as much as anyone. We're still like brothers and we have enormous emotional ties because we were the only four that it all happened to – who went through those ten years.'

From John there was just the cynical comment: 'If you see the Beatles say hello from me to them.'

The start of the seventies had produced a new image for the 'gurus in drag'. In January John and Yoko had gone to spend a few days in Denmark with Yoko's former husband Tony Cox, and her daughter Kyoko, and during their visit they had developed a passing interest in psychic energy and flying saucers. They had also had all their hair cut off with the result that John looked like a GI returning from Vietnam, while without the curtains of hair which covered her forehead and cheek-bones Yoko looked decidedly less enigmatic. No sooner were they back in England than John was in the recording studio making 'Instant Karma', another of his quickie Plastic Ono Band singles. As he put it: 'I wrote it for breakfast, recorded it for lunch and we're putting it out for dinner.' When it was released it had to battle it out with 'Let It Be' in the charts. Again John was being lazy melodically and had borrowed the same chord sequence he had used in 'All You Need Is Love'. But it was an exciting, bouncy, raw rock and roll record.

Depressed by the bickering between lawyers who were beginning the momentous task of working out the finances of Apple, and fed up with the arguments between Allen Klein, who spoke for him, and Lee Eastman, who spoke for Paul, he was again bored. It might almost have been said he was looking for a new Maharishi, when a large book dropped through the post at the Lennons' home at Tittenhurst Park. It was called *Primal Scream*, by American psychiatrist Arthur Yanov, and was to point the way for the Lennons during the next couple of years. The moment Yanov heard that the Lennons were interested in his back-to-babyhood theories he jumped on a plane and was over in Ascot before they could change their minds to convince them that what they really needed was to spend several months with him at his clinic in Los Angeles. They were quickly persuaded. To the probable relief of newspaper headline writers throughout the world, John Lennon, for the first time in eight years, was going into seclusion. He had found a new interest.

The Working-class Hero's
Primal Scream

John Lennon understood perfectly that the Beatles were not themselves the sixties, but merely the biggest manifestation of that extraordinary period. He understood the various social and economic forces which had made their success possible, and he equally realized that the climate was changing quickly in the early seventies. Writer Tom Wolfe later wickedly described the seventies as the 'Me Decade', the time when an obsession with self and narcissim took over from the idealisms of Woodstock and flower power. But Wolfe did not make this observation until the decade was half over. John and Yoko had retreated into personal obsession by the spring of 1970.

Yoko was no stranger to the world of psychology but to John, Arthur Yanov and his primal scream theories were novel as well as fascinating. Basically Freudian, Yanov blamed all neuroses on what he described as 'core experiences', usually moments during childhood which the patient later found too painful to endure and therefore 'took comfort in the comfortable half world of neurosis'. His treatment was to force his patients to relive their early pains and face up to them so that 'they would emerge relieved of their neuroses'.

The Lennons' course in primal therapy began at their Tittenhurst Park home in England, and continued during a four-month sojourn in California, where, having now been granted a temporary visitors' visa to visit the USA they took part in group sessions and lived in a rented house in Bel Air. While there, John described to Charles McCarry, a writer with *Esquire*, the effect the experience was having on them. 'This man's book came in the post and when I read it I thought it was like Newton's apple. "This must be it," I said. But I'd been wrong in the past, with the drugs and the Maharishi – now every fakir who comes out of India tries to ring up the Beatles, you know – so I gave the book to Yoko. She agreed with me, so we came out here.' The therapy was, they thought, helping to build their friendship. 'We were in danger of being, I don't know, Zelda and Scott . . . we were happy and we were close . . . but we would have blown up in a few years, we couldn't have kept up at the pace we were going.'

So the two retreated into their childhood, while the lawyers in England set about ways of breaking up the Beatles' partnership.

By the time they returned to England in August, John was eager to return to the recording studios which had now been completed at Tittenhurst Park. It was a new angry and aggressive Lennon that returned from California, and the sessions were remarkable for the starkness of instrumentation, and directness of the lyrics. This was the Lennon of the seventies. Gone was the gobbledegook of the acid spell, when imagery often stood in for meaning, and gone completely was the elaborate musical scoring of the late sixties. Instead we were now getting bare-faced testimonies. At the start of the 'Me Decade', John Lennon presented us with the first 'Me' album. Ringo, Klaus Voorman and John himself made up the Plastic Ono Band on this occasion. Phil Spector produced the sessions.

When the album was released in the autumn John was visibly nervous and anxious about the reviews. This was the direction in which he wanted to move, but he was half afraid now of not being taken too seriously because of his activities of the past two years. 'I don't want to talk too much about Yanov because it'll sound soft,' he said of primal therapy, 'and people will think, "he's off on another kick again". But a lot of the songs were written after primals, when I'd had an insight into myself.'

The most interesting tracks on the album were 'Mother'

('Mother, you had me, but I never had you'), 'Working-class Hero' and 'God', a litany in which he shed his beliefs in everything from magic to Jesus to the Beatles, ending with the line, 'I just believe in me, Yoko and me, that's reality'.

It was a brave step to make such a totally personal statement, and although it was not as critically successful as his next personal album, *Imagine*, and was criticized because of its bleakness, it was powerful and moving. And the primals had introduced John to a new concept, to which he returned repeatedly in the future – the concept of pain.

Speaking about the lack of imagery on the album, John said: 'It's more like "I Want to Hold Your hand", but now I'm aged thirty. I'm writing this way now because it's the way I feel. I used to say I wouldn't be singing "She Loves You" at thirty but I didn't know I would be singing about my mother. But that was what came out of my mouth when I was trying to write songs. I was doing therapy and going through my life and I just wrote about the important things that had happened to me. Just like any artist. When I was a teenager I wrote poetry, a lot of which was gobbledegook, because I was hiding it from Mimi or perhaps hiding my emotions from myself. Then a bit later on with the Beatles I wrote in a very objective way thinking, "This is the way Goffin and King wrote, so this is the way to write rock and roll." I used to write separately from myself – in the way any artist starts off painting derivatively – until I got embarrassed by it.

'When I wrote "Working-class Hero" I was thinking about all the pain and torture that you go through on stage to get love from this audience who really despise you – in a subtle way. They demand something from you. You go up there like Aunt Sally and have things thrown at you. It's idiots like me who go up there to get tortured – well, it's much easier to be in the audience, isn't it? Anyway the insight I got from that was the anguish I went through to get all this love from all those people who couldn't give it to me. I might just as well have been a comedian getting egg thrown in my face.

'How often did the Beatles enjoy a show? Once in how many weeks of touring – all this about clubs and gigs is a dream, actually more like a nightmare. One show in thirty would give us real satisfaction and you'd go through all kinds of hell to get that. So what was I? A performing flea. And from that I came out with "Working-class Hero". I know I perform of my own choice, but that's the game. I set myself up to get knocked down all the time in the hope that they are going to love me – it's like performing for your parents all the time. All people like me start off with this appalling need for love. The need is greater than what Yoko can give me. Why did I make this record . . . for money or prestige? Fun? It's bloody hard work making a record. I went through six months to write the songs. It's no game. It's bloody tough. At first I'm dying to do it and get in here and do one track and then I think, "Oh Christ I wish I'd never started." It's so hard. It's tough. It's like writing an article. You think at first, "Oh, this is going to be a great one," and then after the first paragraph you think, "Fucking hell, I've got all this to do." I mean you get very, very tired. But that's how Yoko and I help each other. Normally an artist has someone from whom he can suck completely. He says, "I'm the fucking artist, where's my dinner?" and the other person has to be passive and quiet. But Yoko's an artist, too, so she helps in another way. This album is my insight into myself.

'I've never enjoyed writing third-person songs. Most of my best songs are in the first person. I like to write about me. On *Help!* the real meaning of the song was lost because we needed a single and it had to be fast. I got very emotional at the time singing the lyrics. I mean it – whatever I'm singing I don't piss about. If I'm singing "awop-bob-a-looma-awop bam boom" I mean it. But if I've written it myself I really mean it more. *Help!* was a bit poetic. I was in a hell of a state when I wrote that. It's a pretty straightforward diary.'

The album was also criticized for being slight of melody. He also had an answer for that: 'With songs like "Working-class Hero" the words present themselves quicker than I have time to write the tunes, and when the words are good I don't bother with the tune much. I just do it in the most functional way. With some of the old ones like "In My Life" and "Across the Universe" I had the words before the tune, and then almost any tune fits. "Working-class Hero" is derivative of every tune I ever heard. "Mother" [the opening track on the album] is basically the same tune as "You Can't Do That", which was a flip side because "Can't Buy Me Love" was so good. And that was me trying to write, as I still am, that old Sam Cooke hit, "Bring It On Home to Me".'

He was worried at the time that 'Working-class Hero' would cause an uproar because of the line 'till you're so fucking crazy you can't follow their rules', but the climate had changed considerably in the two years since the *Two Virgins* album. This time there was no uproar, although the track did not receive too many radio plays. All the same he refused to change the offending word to 'bloody'.

'That's the way I talk,' he said. 'The word just came out that way. When I was with the Beatles we used to do dirty little things on records. In the middle eight of 'Girl' the others were singing "tit-tit-tit-tit" in the background, and on "Penny Lane" we said "four of fish and finger pie" which is a bit of Liverpool boyhood smut. Then on "Day Tripper" we sang, "She's a prick teaser, she took me half the way there." On "Give Peace a Chance" I say "masturbation" but on the lyric sheet I changed it to "mastication" because I was a coward and I didn't want to be banned again. I'd just been banned for singing "Christ . . . they're gonna crucify me" on "The Ballad of John and Yoko".'

The effect of primal therapy upon John had not been to cure his neuroses but to encourage him to be more waspish than he had been for years. Asked if he was sorry that he did not have more formal education, he fired back aggressively by saying he was *glad* that he had not had more.

'The middle classes are the neurotic ones,' he said. 'The workers have problems about basic things. So I don't want middle-class education in that way. If I'd had a good education I wouldn't have been me. When I was at grammar school I thought I'd go to university because I was a wizard, but I didn't get any GCEs. Then when I was at art school I thought I'd go on to the Slade because I was a wonder, but I never fitted in. I was always a freak.'

It almost seemed that he did protest too much.

The peace campaign of the previous year seemed a very long time ago that autumn. He had allowed a group of Hare Krishna people to live around Tittenhurst Park until eventually he grew tired of their chanting and smiling and threw them out. 'I couldn't get any bloody peace with them walking around all the time,' he would joke against himself occasionally. 'It was all right me going around saying "peace" to everyone. But I wasn't having any myself. Normally I'm very quiet, very delicate. I've always been delicate. I'm not a tough guy. I've had a facade of being tough to protect me from whatever was going on as a child or a teenager or a Beatle. But I'm not like that. I'm not going to waste my life as I was before which is running at 20,000 miles an hour. I have to learn how not to do that, because I don't want to die when I'm forty.'

He still believed in peace, he insisted, but in future he was going to find other ways of expressing his beliefs.

That was a strange and lonely period in the lives of John and Yoko, living out at Tittenhurst Park and often staying in bed all weekend. ('Yes, literally, from Friday night until Monday morning,' said Yoko. 'Sometimes we think we should get up and go for a walk in the grounds, and it's nice when we do, but it takes so much effort that we rarely do it the next day.') They had bought the house in 1969, a beautiful Georgian mansion, set in an estate of seventy hilly acres of heath, groves, woods and massive Oriental trees which were protected by the local council, and where they had created an artificial lake with a rubber lining to keep the water from running away. It was certainly a beautiful place, but it was also empty and remote. An American called Dan Richter and his wife looked after the Lennons, with the help of a couple of secretaries. A cook provided the meals. There were few visitors, and although they would show guests their friendship wall with

137

some pride, and even ask them to sign, it was obviously going to be years before the wall was even partly filled. They had spent hundreds of thousands of pounds on the house and grounds but it was a lonely place. At that time in their lives they seemed almost like a middle-aged or elderly couple who were convalescing after an illness. Their clothes were mainly army surplus, and on their rare ventures into their grounds they would ride around in a small electric buggy, John driving, Yoko cuddled up alongside him. Still John could joke. 'I always wanted to be an eccentric millionaire, and now I am. It was Yoko who changed me. She forced me to become avant garde and take my clothes off when all I wanted to be was Tom Jones. And now look at me.'

Although the house was vast, the few guests they received were entertained either in the kitchen or in an all-purpose room in which the television and stereo speakers stood sentinel at the end of the bed and from which they would greet friends or spend hours making long-distance telephone calls. John's obsession with television and newspapers had never stopped, and as Yoko chattered away he would dreamily watch TV, usually with the sound turned off. He had had an elaborate stereo system built into the room, but he could never get it to work and would end up playing old rock and roll records on a small cheap record player.

He was now the working-class hero at thirty, who had withdrawn from his public life for several months, and was finding that Tittenhurst Park was as alien to him as Kenwood. He wanted to live the good, country, millionaire's life, but it was never going to be possible. All the same, he did stick it out for nearly another year.

In December, while Paul McCartney was beginning High Court procedures to end the Beatles' partnership, John and Yoko flew to New York, 'Yoko's old stomping ground', as John put it. To John, seeing New York with Yoko was like discovering a new way of life. He was intoxicated by it. As a Beatle his visits to New York had been wild carnivals of media hype which had locked the Beatles in their hotel rooms as the fans laid seige. Now Yoko was showing John a completely new side of New York, the New York she had know years earlier of artists, galleries and cosmopolitan liberalism. At Ascot John was the rich eccentric pretending an interest in the English countryside. But in New York he could rediscover the fun of being the freaky art student in the anonymous big city. Of course nothing that John Lennon did made him anonymous, but the bustling activity which he saw around him was seductive. He had shed his Beatle skin: from now on he was to refer to himself repeatedly as an 'artist'. He continually poked fun at the serious critics who had written learned pieces about Beatle records like William Mann who, in a famous review for *The Times* in 1964, discovered aeolian cadences in 'Not a Second Time' ('They were just chords like any other chords,' said John). Nevertheless, he was always flattered to be accepted by serious writers and artists. Throughout the seventies Van Gogh would be mentioned nearly as often as Chuck Berry, and usually in the same breath.

Curiously, a grotesque relic of the days of Beatle-interpreting was thrown in his face that autumn when the lawyer defending Charles Manson in the Sharon Tate murder trial in California requested that John Lennon be called as a witness. Manson was claiming that he had ordered his followers to commit mass murder because a race war was predicted in the lyrics of the Beatles record 'Helter Skelter'. The defence said they needed John to go and explain the lyrics. Unhelpfully, a 'Beatle spokesman' in London said, 'It's like asking Shakespeare to go and explain Macbeth.' It wasn't. 'I won't be there – ever,' said John. Besides, Paul had written the song and it was nothing at all to do with revolution of any kind.

Before the Lennons left the States that winter they made a couple more films. One, called *Up Your Legs*, was a variation on Yoko's bottoms theme. But by now their films were attracting little general interest. During the early and mid-seventies it grew increasingly hard to shock or be controversial, and the Lennons' ventures into the avant garde received scant newspaper coverage.

What *did* shock and was well reported was the long interview with Jann Wenner, published in the magazine *Rolling Stone* in January 1971. This must have been the primal scream which virtually all the Beatle aides had been dreading for years, as John completely spilled the beans on the seedier side of Beatle tours, and talked freely about the groupies, the random sex and the dope which had been kept secret while the lovable four had barnstormed around the world. There were undoubtedly some very difficult domestic scenes as a result of John's revelations both among the Beatle families and those of their retinue, and also among some of the pressmen who had gone with the tours. John didn't tell anything to *Rolling Stone* that was particularly new, although his assertion that the tours were like 'Fellini's *Satyricon*' was a rather grandiose and extravagant way of saying that an awful lot of screwing had taken place. What was new was that a magazine was printing it. Throughout all the years of Beatlemania there had been an unspoken conspiracy of silence by the players, their supporting cast and the press. The more earthy side of touring went unreported. No one wanted to be the one to prick the bubble of Beatle-beatification. Wherever the Beatles had gone there had been girls, hundreds of them. Enough for everybody, press as well.

During much of 1971 it was not so much the tabloid press and music critics who were to write about the Beatles but the normally staid court reporters. After a short trip to Japan to meet Yoko's parents for the first time, John returned to England to find a morass of legal disputes virtually engulfing the Beatles' businesses. The main dispute was caused by Paul McCartney's proceedings in the High Court to dissolve the Beatles' partnership, but there were always several other ancillary cases proceeding simultaneously. There was rancour everywhere. It was even suggested that the Beatles might not be able to pay their income tax, although more than four million pounds had been earned the previous year. Paul claimed that Allen Klein was taking more than his fair share of Beatle profits for himself, and John counter-attacked in a written statement saying that before Klein had arrived Apple had been full of 'spongers and hustlers . . . and that the staff came and went as they pleased and were lavish with money and hospitality'. He added: 'We have since discovered that at around that time two of Apple's cars had completely disappeared and also that we own a house that no one can remember buying.' At the beginning of March the judge put an end to this surreal comedy when he ruled that a receiver should be brought in to manage the Beatles' assets. Klein had been stripped of his power and was on the way out.

In the same month, 'Power to the People', the new Plastic Ono Band record, was released. It was a disappointing bellicose chant, a slogan more than a song.

From the High Court the scene then jumped to a small court in Majorca. It was over a year since John and Yoko had seen Yoko's daughter Kyoko. Yoko became worried about her and traced her to a nursery in Majorca where she was staying with her father. Suddenly the Lennons were being accused of kidnapping the child and they were ordered to appear in court. It was all a misunderstanding. Kyoko was returned to her father and the Lennons spent the next six months chasing Tony Cox through the courts in Texas, New York and the Virgin Islands trying to get custody of her. Nine years later Yoko was to tell an interviewer from *Playboy* magazine that they did indeed kidnap the child, but, when asked who she would rather live with, Kyoko decided in favour of her father. After that summer Kyoko disappeared out of their lives completely.

In July 1971 the Lennons went home to Tittenhurst Park to make what most consider to be John's best record of all. It was the album *Imagine*, and apart from the haunting title theme which will probably endure as the best loved Lennon song ever, and which became a huge hit in Britain when re-issued after his death, it also contained the very moving 'Jealous Guy', 'Oh My Love' and 'How?'. It was an intensely personal record, but on this occasion he and Phil Spector decided to augment the bare sound of the Plastic Ono Band (made up on this occasion of a selection of musicians which included Klaus Voorman on bass, Nicky Hopkins on piano and Jim Keltner on drums).

John knew the album was very, very good. But he was, as usual, nervous about it, and when he played it to friends he suggested that perhaps the single taken from it should be 'Gimme Some Truth', when it was clear to everyone that the song 'Imagine' towered above everything else. When it was pointed out to him how good 'Imagine' was, he would smile and say 'Oh good . . . I like that one, too.' He had worked on the 'imagine theme' many years earlier in collaboration with Paul on 'I'll Get You', but this time he was aided by Yoko's book *Grapefruit*. Later he would suggest that Yoko should have received a credit for her work in conceiving the song.

With this album it seemed that all the diverse spirits which were John Lennon had finally congregated into a dazzling whole. There was the philosopher ('Imagine there's no countries, it isn't hard to do, Nothing to kill or die for, and no religion too'); the romantic ('I was feeling insecure, You might not love me anymore, I was shivering inside'); the cynical wordsmith of 'Gimme Some Truth' ('No short-haired, yellow-bellied son of tricky dicky Is gonna mother-hubbard soft-soap me with just a pocketful of hope'); and then there was the hysterical attack on Paul in 'How Do You Sleep?'. This was where the Lennon rapier wit turned into viciousness with lines such as 'The only thing you done was yesterday, And since you've gone you're just another day', and 'The sound you make is muzak to my ears, You must have learned something in all those years'. John claimed it was in answer to a reference to himself on Paul's *Ram* album, but it was an unkind over-reaction, which a year later he was to admit when he said: 'I went through a period of trying to encourage Paul by writing and saying things which I thought would spur him on. But I think they were misunderstood. That was how I wrote "How Do You Sleep?". I suppose it was a bit hard on him. But that was how I felt when I recorded it.'

The appearance of George Harrison on *Imagine* prompted

some pundits of the time to predict a closening of relationships between all the ex-Beatles, but George was, in fact, to be the cause of one of the biggest rows that John and Yoko ever had. In August 1971, George organized a concert at Madison Square Gardens in aid of the people of Bangladesh, and invited Ringo, Bob Dylan, Eric Clapton, Bill Preston and many other musicians including John and Paul to take part.

Paul did not accept but John did. Then the day before the concert there was a row between George and John over Yoko. Yoko wanted to appear on stage. George did not want her. Eventually John gave in, and flew back to London leaving Yoko to follow some hours later. It was almost back to the days of the *White Album* when George, together with Paul and Ringo, had not wanted Yoko in the studio. Yoko felt that John should have stood up for her against George. John, as usual in these situations, resolved it by walking away from the dispute himself. Sometimes he must have felt he had a lot to put up with facing Yoko's aggressiveness, but he never publicly uttered a single word of reproach towards her.

Back in England they made friends again, and the row was forgotten as their political consciousness was raised once more. They joined in a march of protest against internment in Northern Ireland on one day, and on the next day gave £1000 to a fighting fund to keep open the Upper Clyde Shipbuilders in Glasgow and prevent unemployment. Politically they were dilettantes, but forever generous.

And then suddenly, after making an appearance on a Michael Parkinson chat show on BBC television one Saturday night in September, they slipped out of England for the last time. There was no big decision. It was as though John Lennon were simply shedding another skin from himself. At first they no doubt intended to return at some point and for a while staff were kept on at Tittenhurst Park, but gradually all the belongings they needed were shipped out to New York. A stage in the life of John Lennon was over. When he had left Liverpool he never felt any need to go back; when he left his home in St George's Hill Estate he left behind rooms full of memorabilia. Now he was leaving behind him a home which would later be valued at over a million pounds. He had simply lost interest in it, although the workmen still had not finished, and the ornamental lake had only just been completed.

A few months earlier he and Yoko had shown guests the carpet which they had had specially imported from communist China. Now it was forgotten. As John had bored with the Beatles, now he was bored by England. In New York he was taken seriously as a rich, free-thinking artist, rather than as the Beatle who had become silly. New York offered him a new identity and a new freedom. It was cosmopolitan. Yoko would find acceptance easier there. Eight years later, when asked why he had never returned to England, they would reply that he intended to at some time, and that England wasn't going to go away. It would always be there when he decided to come back.

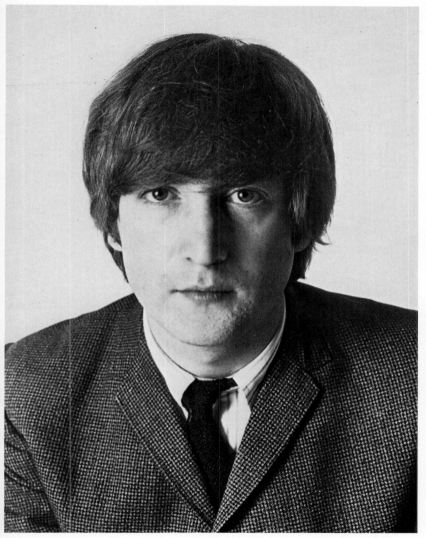

40. 'What does Beatle mean?' an American interviewer once asked John. 'It's just a name . . . like Shoe,' he replied. 'We could have been called The Shoes.'

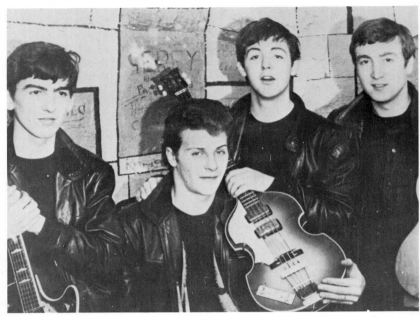

41. An early Cavern picture that shows Pete Best who played drums before the arrival of Ringo.

42. In the spring of 1963 the Beatles were presented with a silver disc to mark a quarter of a million sales of 'Please, Please Me'. Producer George Martin rightfully joined the celebrations.

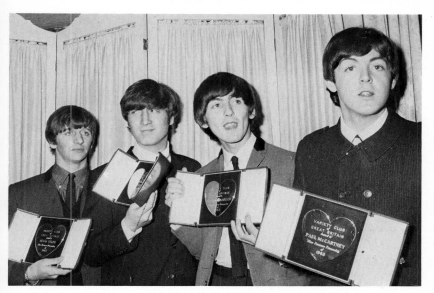

43. Awards were showered on them. At the Variety Club of Great Britain lunch they were named Show Business Personalities of 1963.

44. 'What excuse do you have for your collar-length hair?' asked an American interviewer. 'It just grows out of your head,' replied John. (Miami, 1964)

45. Paul shows Ed Sullivan what a guitar is during their first visit to New York in 1964. Brian Epstein watches in the background.

46. At the Carl Alan Awards in 1964 the Duke of Edinburgh offered to swap a copy of one of his books for a copy of John's *In His Own Write*. John agreed. 'You don't know what you're letting yourself in for,' replied the Duke. Neither did he.

47. A familiar scene at London Airport in the mid-sixties as the Beatles return from one of their world tours.

48. The ultimate accolade of respectability came when they were presented with their MBEs by the Queen in 1965. John later returned his in protest against British involvement in the war in Nigeria, their support of the Americans in Vietnam – and because 'Cold Turkey' was slipping down the charts.

49. A fan gets on stage in Rome and pursues John. He was sometimes frightened by the hysteria of fans.

50. The end of live appearances is in sight as the Beatles go off on tour of Japan in 1966.

51. Wearing a sporran and Afghan jacket, John introduced the Press to the world of Sergeant Pepper in June 1967 at a party in Brian Epstein's home.

52. The last occasion on which John and Paul were to spend any
time alone together after the arrival of Yoko was during this trip to
New York in 1968 when they announced the setting up of their
Apple business.

53. Fans gathered together in New York and Liverpool on Sunday, 17 December 1980, to pay homage: (*above*) in New York they played and sang 'Give Peace a Chance'; (*below*) in Liverpool it was 'She Loves You'. In attitude the fans were more than 3000 miles apart.

III

New York

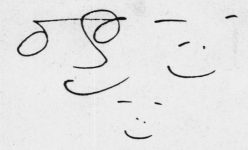

Mind Games
in New York City

By the time John Lennon set up home in New York in 1971 he was already savouring the freedom of the anti-hero. So far as he was concerned the Beatles were a part of history. He had shed that life forever. He was like an art student at thirty-one. He wanted to do all the things that he had missed while being imprisoned inside his Beatle shell. He wanted to meet people who were non-musicians, and he deliberately sought the Bohemian world of artists, poets and underground political activists. In Britain he had tried to destroy his own myth, but living as an eccentric millionaire in Tittenhurst Park had made that impossible. Now he was to take his myth into the streets of New York and Greenwich Village and tear it apart with poor records and radical propaganda.

During his first few months in New York John told the *Daily Mail*: 'This city has become the centre of the artistic world. It's really great to live here with all these talented people. New York is more like Liverpool than London. Like Liverpudlians, New Yorkers are tough people who live close to the water and have a special way of speaking. As a kid I was brought up on Americana. We watched films from the US and drank Coke . . . after living in Britain for thirty years I'd like to try it here. A few decades abroad never hurt anyone.'

At first John and Yoko set up home on the seventeenth floor of the staid St Regis Hotel, where they proceeded to amass recording and film-editing equipment, records and clothes. They were living out of dozens of trunks as their personal belongings were being shipped over from England. John had been granted a six-month non-renewable visa and he looked as though he was going to pack every day full of activity.

In October he and Yoko held a huge exhibition at Syracuse University, in up-state New York. In essence it was do-it-yourself time, and friends and artists alike were requested to offer exhibits. One memorable piece was a huge block of ice in the shape of the letter T which was slowly melting and which was titled 'Iced Tea'; another was a corroded shell of a Volkswagen from Andy Warhol; there was a glass maze to get lost in, and a messages box to get found in. Even Ringo turned up with his expression of permanent bewilderment.

This was Yoko's first big exhibition in America and John was sparing no one's energies in promoting his wife as a serious artist. He said: 'I've bet Yoko a thousand dollars that somebody somewhere will write an article which really understands her work before the end of this year. I don't mean just a complimentary article, or any of that intellectual bullshit like I've had about my albums by people who like them but don't understand them. I mean an article by someone who really knows what she's talking about. If nobody writes it, I'll have to write it myself . . .'

The event was called This Is Not Here. Yoko explained it in this way: 'I'm trying to get across the idea that the art is in the people who come to see it. It's like saying, "you are important, not the objects." It's the people's reactions that are important. Everyone is an artist, but some people are more intimidated by art than others. No one can say that Ringo's contribution is less important than that of Andy Warhol or Jasper Johns or John Cage.'

John would listen to all this, nodding aggressively. But it did place him in a slightly ambivalent position. Convinced of his own genius, artistry and natural superiority ('I used to be quite surprised that I hadn't become a famous painter,' he would say with a mocking grin), the democratization of art to the level of 'we are all artists' must have fitted uneasily into his scheme of things.

During the three days the Lennons spent in Syracuse Yoko held a birthday party for John in their hotel suite. The whole town and university campus was jumping with excitement as John and Yoko fought through the crowds, and several quite tough bodyguards, hired by the Allen Klein organization to look after the couple during the weekend, helped block off the corridors to the suite, with some help from the local police.

The guests at the birthday party included Yoko's sister Setsuko and her Swiss boyfriend, Ringo and his wife Maureen, Phil Spector, Klaus Voorman, Yoko's secretary in New York, May Pang, a few Apple employees from New York and a group of Klein employees and hangers-on. John was in high spirits, but surprisingly nervous when someone passed him his guitar and asked him to sing. Surrounded by people he knew well, he felt embarrassed. At last he was coaxed into performing his old rock and roll repertoire of 'That'll Be The Day', 'Blue Suede Shoes', 'Lawdy Miss Clawdy' and dozens of others. Even Ringo sang 'Yellow Submarine'. It was a happy, good-natured party. There was some wine and birthday cake, and John did several versions of 'Give Peace a Chance', fitting the words around the names of the assembled guests.

But there was another side to the party. In the next room, unknown to John and most people at the party, some of the drivers and security men were taking it in turns to screw some doped-up girl who they had allowed up on the promise that she could meet John Lennon. The next day when John was told of the happenings in the next room he looked puzzled for a while. Then he said quietly: 'Don't tell Yoko, will you?'

John was always very protective of Yoko, which was ironic because before she met him Yoko had been a very tough self-reliant person. It was indeed her independence which had attracted him most. She had never conformed to the standard set by the other Beatle wives of only being seen in public when they had had their hair done.

The strain of being together twenty-four hours a day for the past four years began to become apparent as soon as the Lennons moved to New York. Late in 1971 they decided they wanted to view an apartment in the Dakota building, the Gothic block on Central Park West to which they were to eventually move in 1973. Knowing that the other residents of the block were considered rich and conservative, John dressed in a suit. Yoko, on the other hand, wore hot pants and a shirt unbuttoned down the front. Suddenly John began viciously to berate her in front of a friend, saying that she looked like 'a tart and a fucking whore' and insisting that she change into something more suitable. Without a murmur, Yoko left the room to return in something more formal. John's attack had been cruel and humiliating. Then suddenly, within minutes, he was joking again as he opened a letter from a university in Tennessee offering him sixty thousand dollars just to talk to the students. 'Just imagine,' he said in amazement, 'sixty thousand dollars and I don't even have to sing. Daft, isn't it?'

During their first months in New York the Lennons threw themselves into a turmoil of activity. They recorded a new single, 'Happy Christmas (War is Over)', they performed in a benefit show in Michigan, and they co-hosted the Mike Douglas nightly TV show for a week, playing with Chuck Berry one night. John was overjoyed with this: 'Just imagine *me* playing with Chuck Berry on TV,' he said, his mouth open with admiration.

With the intensity of the war in Vietnam showing few signs of lessening, it was an intensely political period and John soon found himself being lionized by the radical politicists of the early seventies New York scene, people like Jerry Rubin, Abbie Hoffman and John Sinclair.

By the end of 1971 the Lennons had taken their first permanent home in New York, a two-room loft in Greenwich Village, where they greeted pressmen and underground politicos from their huge antique bed. Although John had always denied an interest in politics when he was a Beatle he had actually always been lying. He was intensely interested in politics, and an acute observer of the class system, but he had the weakness of the dilettante, sometimes a ranting fanatic and then quickly bored with all the cant and verbiage that is part of politics. It was during this period that he was to make quite positively his worst album ever, a hotch-potch of sloganeering which he called *Some Time in New York City*, on which he was backed by a band called Elephant's Memory. It was disappointing because the sparkle and wit for wordplay had been replaced by rhetoric. In the *Imagine* album of a year earlier he had been full of hope; now he was suddenly taking sides in condemnation, particularly about Ireland. 'Why the hell are the English there anyway, / As they kill with God on their side! / Blame it all on the kids and the IRA! / As the bastards commit genocide,' he sang in 'The Luck of the Irish', while in another song he became positively violent: 'Internment is no answer, / It's those mothers' turn to burn.'

The most interesting track on the album was 'Woman is the Nigger of the World', which had been the headline to an article written about Yoko in the London magazine, *Nova*. Right from her Sarah Lawrence days Yoko had been interested in the feminist movement and since her meeting with John she had been slowly educating him in her beliefs. But again John overstated his case with the song, with the result that as a single it was banned nearly everywhere and was only a minor hit. Eight years later he would return to the subject with the haunting 'Woman' on his last album, and make a far more effective statement without any of the vitriol or disgust, a disgust which, considering his personal behaviour, was at the least hypocritical at that time.

The early seventies were the days when Gloria Steinhem, Kate Millett and Germaine Greer competed with each other to express most stridently the case of women's liberation. In many ways there was an irony here. John was reacting to newspaper headlines and articles written by educated middle-class women to be read by other educated middle-class women. For a short time he had become a banner bearer for a fashionable movement which he hardly understood, and for a section of a class he had always professed to despise.

The real trouble was that John was posing. He had picked up on the feeling of the moment and without fully digesting any of it was busy making statements using all the emotive words of the time – 'concentration camps', 'pigs', 'genocide'. Compared with the biting, spiky sarcasm of his anti-war song 'The Continuing Story of Bungalow Bill' from three years earlier, the effect of 'Some Time in New York City' was glib and whining. Writer Tom Wolfe might have included John Lennon in his essay on the radical chic, except that John was not being particularly chic about his radicalism as he would hang out around Max's Kansas City in the Village, always the centre of post-Yippie attention.

Still, his heart was in the right place if his music wasn't, and in the summer of 1972 he and Yoko did two charity concerts at Madison Square Gardens in aid of homes for handicapped children. Altogether it was estimated that the Lennons helped raise £700,000 for charity during 1972.

During the spring and summer of 1972 John's boundless faith in human nature, and correspondingly his interest in minor political activists, was delivered a crushing blow when a one-time 'friend' from England, Michael Abdul Malik, better known to the British press as Michael X, was arrested and charged with murder in Trinidad. John's association with Malik had begun in 1969 when Malik had tapped him for funds to set up a centre for 'black culture' in London. Malik had an appalling reputation as a strong man and bully for a London slum landlord of the sixties called Peter Rachman. But somehow Malik managed to convince John that he had turned over a new leaf and was going to represent and work for the underprivileged London West Indian community. John, along with other gullible, but no less generous, benefactors took Malik at his word. Property was bought and The Black House was set up. Malik could be extremely plausible and charming.

Within a few months, however, the venture was in ruins, as a fire swept The Black House and Malik was arrested and charged with robbery and demanding money with menaces. Having been jailed three years earlier for inciting racial hatred, Malik was determined not to risk prison again and in January 1971 he jumped bail (which had been provided by the Lennons) and flew to Trinidad where he set up a small commune. On one occasion the Lennons visited Malik there, but in February 1972 Malik became a wanted man after the commune, too, was burnt down. This time, however, he left behind two corpses, one a friend and employee and the other the neurotic daughter of an English former Conservative Member of Parliament who had been staying at the commune with her American black-power boyfriend Hakim Jamal. Malik was eventually traced to Guyana, arrested and taken back to Trinidad to stand trial for murder. Typically the only people to offer him any funds for his defence costs were the Lennons. They sent a gift of £1000. Malik was found guilty and condemned to death. The Lennons sent a plea for leniency. No matter what Malik had done they were, they said, praying for him. In 1973 Malik was hanged for two murders.

During their association with Malik the Lennons had behaved with complete openness and generosity towards him, his wife and children. John said later that his guilt about being rich and yet working class always meant that he was wide open to anyone who could strike that very touchy nerve.

The most common newspaper headline concerning John Lennon between 1972 and 1975 was in connection with his battle with the United States Immigration and Naturalization Service. Technically the Federal authorities were using John's conviction on the 1968 marijuana charge as a reason for having him thrown out of the States, but the lengths to which they went was out of all proportion to the small misdemeanour he had committed. Being John Lennon, he was not prepared to go without a long-drawn-out fight through the courts, and, being America, that is exactly what happened, at an estimated cost to John of nearly half a million pounds.

In 1972 John went on the Dick Cavett television show and claimed that there was a conspiracy against him, that he was being trailed and that his phone was tapped. All of this seemed highly melodramatic at the time and extremely unlikely. But it was almost certainly true. As Watergate subsequently showed, the paranoia of the Nixon administration knew no bounds. The association John had made with Jerry Rubin and John Sinclair worried the administration who thought he might be used as a tool for political disruption. All of this eventually came to light in Jack Anderson's syndicated newspaper column in 1974, when John was once again fighting a rearguard action around yet another order for his deportation. The very idea that the Attorney General of the United States, the unhappy John Mitchell, should have believed that John Lennon could be a potentially disruptive influence and rallying point in anti-war protests indicates the warmth with which John had been adopted by American youth.

For four years, however, the insecurity of John's position in the States played havoc with his personal life. He was now trapped inside America. He knew that if he ever left he would never get back in. The pressures were piling up on him. It was time for a new album, but he was not particularly inspired. The result was *Mind Games*, a vast improvement over *Some Time in New York City*, but short on melody and wit. It was only moderately successful. He was beginning to worry now about his failure to create hit records in the way he had once found so effortless, and worry also about the prospect of middle age.

Just after his thirty-third birthday in 1973, John and Yoko separated. It was the first time they had been apart for more than a couple of days since 1968. Their parting was not without some acrimony. They were now living in the first of their apartments in the Dakota (they eventually owned seven) and John, after singing with so much passion a year before about the terrible way men treated women, proceeded to do just that to Yoko, publicly humiliating her by going off with other women at parties, and eventually disappearing to Los Angeles with Yoko's secretary, a New York Chinese girl called May Pang.

It was always difficult to understand John's attraction for May.

154

She had been part of the Lennon entourage since 1971, a happy goffer in jeans and T-shirt, who was always at Yoko's beck and call. She was pretty but not beautiful, and socially and intellectually she didn't enter Yoko's universe. She had once worked for the Allen Klein organization, and she certainly knew her way around rock and roll, but she was no lasting soul-mate for John.

A few weeks before his death John explained in several interviews that Yoko had kicked him out because he was behaving so badly. At first he thought, 'Whoopee! Bachelor life! Whoopee!' But it didn't turn out quite like that.

In California he rented a house on the beach at Santa Monica, a huge star-type place on the Pacific Coast Highway which had formerly belonged to Peter Lawford and where May would entertain friends with the gossip that it was the house where the Kennedys had met Marilyn Monroe when they were in town. It was actually a terrible place of vast pool tables, swimming pools, and acres of pastel-coloured carpets, across which were scattered all the ephemera of the rock and roll musician's life: guitar cases, amplifiers, cigarette cartons, broken strings, drum sticks, beer cans.

In Los Angeles John and May quickly took on new personalities. For years she had been the runaround girl in New York. Now she could behave as the mistress of the house, and the Mexican servants cooked and served at her behest. Suddenly she was glamorous. John went on an orgy of self-destruction. He would refer to it later as his eighteen-month lost weekend in which he joined Harry Nilsson and Keith Moon in heavy drinking binges. He said that it seemed to be like a competition to see who could drink himself to death first. Keith Moon was the winner.

The worse the aggravation from the Immigration Department, the more John would drink, and the worse his behaviour became. The nightmare of many days was waking up to read in the newspapers about how appallingly he had behaved the previous night. For months the papers were full of his lunatic behaviour. He had dropped all his politico-activist friends and was living out an existence as the wild man of rock. As though he didn't have enough problems, the relationship with former Beatles' manager Allen Klein was now diminishing quickly, while the Beatles and Apple settlement looked no nearer to solution. As a friend remarked at the time: 'The lawyers of the world should erect a statue to the Beatles for having kept them in employment for so long in trying to sort out Apple affairs.'

John's first venture in Los Angeles was to produce a rock and roll album with Phil Spector. For years he had been writing all of his own material, having to worry about whether the lyrics were meaningful enough to live up to the Lennon legend. Now he just wanted to get back, right back to his Cavern days, when he sang rock and roll for the fun of it. Phil Spector had been one of the great record producers of the sixties with his renowned 'wall of sound', and John suggested to him that he should sing just like the Ronnettes and Chiffons had done a decade earlier. At first all went well, and five good tracks were produced. But inevitably the two soon fell out. If Lennon was crazy, then Spector had to be crazier. Before he knew it, the sessions had run into all kinds of legal problems about who owned the tapes; Warner Brothers, to whom Spector was under contract, or EMI's American subsidiary, Capitol, which still held John's contract. It was a typical rock and roll confusion. Once again lawyers stepped in to sort out the situation. In the meantime John got drunker and drunker and took to producing an album for Harry Nilsson.

Talking about his lost weekend to Barbara Graustark of *Newsweek*, John said: 'I was like an elephant in a zoo, aware that it is trapped but not able to get out. It was an extension of the craziness that I'd been doing with the Beatles in Hamburg and Liverpool, but it had been covered up then by the people surrounding me.'

As the immigration and business problems multiplied (he was now being sued by Allen Klein), John continued to flit back and forth between New York and Los Angeles, calling Yoko constantly at their home in the Dakota. But it was not until the end of 1974 that the two were reconciled. According to John, Yoko simply would not let him back until she thought that he was ready. Without her he was tearing himself to pieces, and everybody else who happened to be around him. At one famous incident at the Troubadour Club in Los Angeles he was bodily thrown out by the management after constantly interrupting the Smothers Brothers' act with wisecracks. When followed by a girl photographer, he aimed a punch in her direction only to find himself accused of assault. The incident was dropped after he sent a gift in apology.

Trying to make a record with Harry Nilsson was difficult, too. All the musicians were living in John's house and it quickly became completely chaotic. 'It was a madhouse,' he told *Newsweek*. 'And I realized that I was in charge.' In fact the bills were being sent to him. Suddenly he realized that he had to stop drinking or go under. He stopped and began to pull himself together.

During the first few months of their separation John and Yoko had obviously considered divorce. Yoko had more than adequate grounds. But publicly neither of them ever criticized the other. John began to spend more and more time in New York. While living in Los Angeles he had written one outstanding song, 'Nobody Loves You When You're Down and Out', a totally autobiographical mood-song, and he was anxious to record it properly. In New York he gathered his favourite post-Beatle musicians around him – Klaus Voorman on bass, Nicky Hopkins on piano and Jim Keltner on drums – and went to work on a new album, *Walls and Bridges*. It was undoubtedly the best thing he had recorded since *Imagine*. Gone were all the political chants. He was singing from within himself again. In 'Scared' he worried about his age:

I'm tired of being so alone,
No place to call my own,
Like a rollin' stone;

on 'Steel and Glass' he turned his fury on someone believed to be the now out-of-favour Allen Klein, just as he had once attacked Paul McCartney:

Your mother left you when you were small,
But you're gonna wish you wasn't born at all,
he sang, and then,

Your teeth are clean, but your mind is capped.
You leave your smell like an alley cat.

But although the album produced two hit songs, 'Whatever Gets You Through the Night' and 'Dream Number Nine', it was 'Nobody Loves You When You're Down and Out' which captured his mood accurately:

Everybody's hustling for a buck and a dime,
I'll scratch your back and you'll knife mine.

He had hoped that someone like Frank Sinatra would record the song, but it was too personal to him to be covered by anyone else. Even his voice was husky and tired, the voice of a man who has been through a lot of hard nights. Although May Pang was the production co-ordinator on the record, her days of consort were nearly over. Following a concert at Madison Square Gardens in November 1974 when John joined Elton John on stage to sing 'Whatever Gets You Through the Night' and 'Lucy in the Sky with Diamonds', John and Yoko were reconciled at a backstage meeting. That night he went home with her. They were never to be apart again. When asked about the reconciliation he said quite simply: 'The separation didn't work out . . . I feel as though I've been on Sinbad's voyage and I've battled all those monsters and I've got back.'

Of course there were still all kinds of business problems to be sorted out but now, with the help of the revelations about the Nixon administration's interference in the vexed question of his visa, it began to look as though the fight was at last going John's way. A few weeks earlier he finished off his *Rock 'n' Roll* album of standards (on which May Pang was given the credit of 'Production Co-ordinator and Mother Superior', a compliment he had once reserved for Yoko), and he now set about settling some of his other differences, mainly with Lew Grade's company, ATV Music, which had been publishing all Lennon and McCartney material since it had taken over Northern Songs in 1969. Under a new deal he was made a co-publisher of all his own material from 1972 onwards. Included in the agreement was a big cash settlement of over a million pounds each for John and Paul. Evidence that John was pleased with the outcome of the deal was apparent when he appeared in a television show in 1976, marking Grade's seventieth birthday.

Then in the spring of 1975 a few of Yoko's friends received a short handwritten card through the post one morning. It read simply: 'Here's a hard one for you to take. Not only have John and Yoko got back together, but they are expecting a baby due in October.' Since Yoko had had at least three previous miscarriages and was then aged forty-one, it looked like a premature celebration. But this time everything went well. Their baby Sean Ono Lennon was born on 9 October 1976, two days after the US Court of Appeals had ruled that the British law under which John had been convicted was unjust by US standards. His fight to remain in the United States was practically over. The following July the Immigration Service said they no longer objected to his presence in the United States after listening to character references from Gloria Swanson and Norman Mailer. After a five-year battle John Lennon became a legal resident of the United States.

The reformation in John's character was complete. The birth of Sean made him feel 'as high as the Empire State Building', he said. They had had so many difficulties in starting a family before that he had virtually given up on the possibility. 'An English doctor had told me that there was something wrong with my sperm because of the way I'd been abusing my body,' John told the BBC. 'But then we went to visit a little Japanese acupuncture guy in San Francisco and he said, "No . . . everything all right. You give up drink and drugs. And you get baby." So I did. And it worked.'

Cleanup Time for
Greta Hughes and/or
Howard Garbo

On 1 April 1970 the following news item was offered by me to the newsdesk of the London *Evening Standard*:

John and Yoko Lennon today entered the London Clinic for a series of sex-change operations which, if successful, would make them the first married couple in history to completely reverse their marital roles.

If the massive hormone injections are successful Lennon will become a woman, while Yoko Ono will become a man. The Lennons want, I understand, to become the world's first unisex family.

Special surgeons are being flown in from Los Angeles later today to help with the operations, while a special drug known only to a certain caste of Tibetan monk, is being prepared at a secret laboratory in Catford.

From their suite in the clinic John Lennon told me this morning: 'We are doing it to demonstrate once and for all our complete love for each other. We are doing it for peace and because "Instant Karma" is slipping down the charts.'

Said Yoko: 'Yes, yes.'

The world now waits to hear the results of these fantastic moments in the history of mankind. With luck on their side, today's momentous developments should open up all kinds of permutations on the future of family life in the modern age.

It was, of course, an April Fool's Day hoax which amused the Lennons enormously and although not printed on the day was later published as part of an interview with them. But as it turned out, the sentiments behind the hoax were to be extraordinarily accurate. The birth of Sean finally converted John to feminism, not in the strident sloganeering way of 'Woman is the Nigger of the World', but in a caring sense. He actually wanted to set about looking after the baby himself. All his life he had been the tough guy: now he was to change completely. He took up the role of the househusband with a zeal known only to the convert. Gradually a new lifestyle was developed in the Lennon household. Yoko put it this way: 'I had the baby, but I'm not a very good mother at bringing up my children. John loved to be with Sean all the time, so I got on with the business side of things, and John ran the house.' It was a complete role reversal, and John loved it.

Gradually the bitternesses of the previous years faded away, and one by one the links with the past went, too. One of the biggest blows was the killing by police in Los Angeles of John's friend, the former road manager to the Beatles, Mal Evans. Mal, known to the whole Beatle entourage as the Gentle Giant, had joined them in the very early days and stayed loyal until well after the break-up. When John and Yoko played in Totonto it was Mal who organized their appearance; when George did the Bangladesh concert, Mal was again needed. Gradually his function faded as there were fewer gigs and less to do around Apple, and eventually he became a record producer in Los Angeles. Then one night he got stoned and began waving an air pistol around. The Los Angeles Police Department were called to his house and, seeing the Gentle Giant waving what looked like a lethal weapon, they opened fire and shot him dead. It was the most horrible of mistakes. Despite being nearly six foot three inches tall and massively framed, Mal had always avoided fights at all costs when he was protecting the Beatles from the worldwide frenzy. He was the single member of the whole Beatles entourage who was never criticized by any one of the Beatles, and he was undoubtedly the most loyal of their many staff. His death affected John, like the other three Beatles, very deeply. Big Mal was a warm memory of their youth. As John would say later, he saw a lot of death in his life.

The period from 1976 until 1980 will always be remembered as the time John Lennon became a recluse. He would joke about it, referring to himself as Greta Hughes or Howard Garbo, enjoying hearing the rumours that he had locked himself up in the Dakota, that he was growing his fingernails and was refusing to see anyone. This was not true. He was simply refusing to talk to the press and not making any records or personal appearances. For the first time since he was twenty-two he was not under contract to anyone and he was enjoying the freedom. 'Life doesn't end when you stop subscribing to *Billboard*,' he would say to those who questioned his new privacy.

The withdrawal into his home and family was not a sudden event, but took place gradually over a couple of years. In 1976 he wrote the song 'Fame' with David Bowie, and he still regularly saw friends when they were passing through New York. At one time Paul and Linda McCartney got into the habit of popping in to see the Lennons fairly regularly until one day John opened the door to find Paul standing there with a guitar and snapped peevishly at him: 'Would you just mind *calling* before you come round. I've had a hard day with the baby, you know.'

Paul was actually quite hurt. He was as liable as anyone to be stung by the fabled Lennon rapier wit. After that the two hardly saw each other again.

Much as been made of John's role as househusband, but it must always be remembered that John Lennon was a very rich househusband and, under the business management of Yoko, getting increasingly richer. So although he spent a great deal of time with Sean and around the house, Sean also had a nanny, and of course there were the usual cooks and domestic helps to run the home. At the same time he did make a conscious decision to give himself over to taking care of his son until Sean was five, believing in the Jesuits' boast that those are the most formative years of a man's life.

Of course John was enjoying himself, too. Yoko would tell how she liked to be getting on with business, but John was happy just playing with Sean, getting him up and dressed in the morning, fixing his breakfast before handing him over to his nanny. Because of touring he had almost completely missed Julian's early childhood and he was keen not to miss Sean's. He also learned how to cook (he boasted he baked a loaf of bread every day) and that he learned to do all the chores of the housewife. But again it must be stressed: the rich housewife.

When John wasn't playing with Sean he was reading. He had once had no time for reading, but in his five years' seclusion he became an avid reader, devouring everything anthropological he could lay his hands on, following the news carefully (he took an airmail edition of the *Guardian* every day) and even reading some novels. In addition he taught himself Japanese. In many respects John had always been a frustrated intellectual, so in the late seventies he began to catch up on years of educational neglect. 'I read everything on everything,' he told *Newsweek* in September 1980, stressing that he was particularly interested in ancient history. His domestic activities as a househusband may have made good headlines, but his time spent studying was equally important to him. These were reflective years, times when he could look back on his Beatle myth with affection. It is likely that they were the happiest years he ever had. For the first time ever, the pressure was off him, and he had a good manager, in the form of Yoko, to take care of business for him. He had never enjoyed business: Yoko did, as she had always enjoyed chess. John never became the recluse of legend. Auntie Mimi still received the regular jokey, silly phone calls, only now he was telling her things about Sean. He wrote letters to old friends full of the old puns and wordplay typed out on his IBM and signed with the affectionate little cartoon scribble of the two faces of John and Yoko, now joined by a third for Sean.

Realizing that Sean would have to go to school at the age of five,

John's behaviour was geared to getting as much out of those first five years as was possible. He returned to the macrobiotic diet which he had dabbled with years earlier, he lost weight, and he took to walking Sean in his pram in Central Park. He really was an eccentric millionaire now, but apparently a very happy one.

Yoko, meanwhile, was displaying an extraordinary business acumen. At the beginning of 1977 she settled a long-running dispute between the Beatles and Allen Klein. It was, she said, the first time she ever got any praise for anything. From there she moved into dairy farming and real estate, always investing and reinvesting. 'Property is the best thing to have during times of inflation,' she said as she proceeded to buy up more and more apartments in the Dakota, four farms in the Catskills, a mansion by the sea on Long Island and the Vanderbilt's home in Palm Beach, Florida. Then, there were the cows. One estimate published in *Playboy* suggested that the Lennons owned sixty million dollars' worth of dairy cows by 1980. Yoko did not deny this figure, but neither did she confirm it. What was certain was that she did sell a prize cow for a quarter of a million dollars. 'Only Yoko could get a quarter of a million dollars for a cow,' laughed John in admiration. Neither John nor Yoko drank milk, anyway.

In many respects Sean now took over the role of constant companion to John, leaving Yoko to get on with business in her office, with the help of her assistants and secretaries. And John and Sean would go off to the Catskills for days to play, leaving Yoko in Manhattan.

John also used his five years out of the public eye to travel. Once he had been awarded his green card and was able to travel freely in and out of the United States, he took to travelling again. He visited Japan, the Caribbean, Hong Kong, Singapore, South Africa. Sometimes he went with Yoko, sometimes alone. The Hong Kong trip was her idea. Since he had become famous in 1963 John had always had people to do everything for him, simple everyday things like booking airline tickets, hiring cars, buying the daily necessities of life. At Yoko's suggestion John went off to Hong

Kong by himself to learn to live how everybody else lived. Hardly anyone recognized him, and he enjoyed the freedom of being simply a part of the mass of people. He enjoyed doing things for himself. It was a new experience. He told *Newsweek*: 'The king is always killed by his courtiers, not by his enemies. The king is overfed, overdrugged, overindulged, anything to keep the king tied to his throne. Most people in that position never wake up. They either die mentally or physically or both.' He was referring obliquely both to Elvis and to the way he had been himself.

In June 1979 the Lennons again caused some public amusement when they took a full-page advertisement in the *New York Times* proclaiming their love for each other, and ending with the PS, 'We noticed that three angels were looking over our shoulders when we wrote this.' But there was none of the vitriol which such a statement would have provoked a decade earlier. The world now had an open affection for the couple who had endured so much aggravation.

Although both John and Yoko later said that they got on better during this period than ever before, the differences in their lifestyles were quite pronounced. Yoko became obsessed with her collection of ancient Egyptian art and numerology, while John did some painting, listened to a lot of Muzak and classical music, watched television, and kept a juke box full of hit records he liked, some early Elvis like 'Hound Dog' ('Sean thinks it's about chasing rabbits') and some more current records by Olivia Newton John and Donna Summer. While Yoko sat downstairs in her white-cloud-painted office, talking on the telephone, John would be upstairs. Over his bed hung an unplayed guitar. By the side of the bed were the usual amplifiers and headphones. A lot of time, he would say later, was spent watching the cars go by, watching the people in Central Park. It was a time for day-dreaming, the one pastime of which he never grew tired. He never went to night clubs like Studio 54, and he never watched other artists perform. He had no interest in keeping up with New York social life at any level. He was content in his own home and family.

Although he may have been seen less in public, John lost none of his public extravagance or generosity during these years. He donated his special psychedelically painted Rolls-Royce, estimated to be worth £70,000, to the Smithsonian Institute in Washington; he was a tipper on a grand scale (twenty dollars for the doorman every time the car door was opened for him) and he made various donations to charity, one being for a thousand dollars to help provide the New York City Police with bullet-proof vests. He spent money lavishly on cars, he bought an aeroplane, and invested in jewellery and furs. Then, last of all, before he again entered public life he bought a sixty-foot yacht, hired a five-man crew and sailed with Sean to Bermuda.

The finances of the Beatles have had lawyers and tax accountants puzzling over them for the best part of twenty years, so this is no place for a quick summary. John himself had no real idea of how much he was worth, but he did not deny the New York *Daily Post*'s suggestion that his assets could be valued at over 150 million dollars. John's financial situation received a huge financial boost in 1977 with the unfreezing of the Beatles' assets following the break-up of the Beatles' partnership in 1975. That would have accounted for a lump sum payment of several million pounds in back royalties. In addition his income as a composer was estimated to earn him at least five million pounds a year, every year. Although the Beatles had stopped recording together in 1970, EMI and Capitol continued to repackage compilation albums of their songs right through the seventies. Under Brian Epstein's management the Beatles had not been on high royalties. But during the seventies EMI increased their percentages considerably, with a little nudging from Allen Klein, who, after all, was due twenty per cent of all earnings during his two years of stewardship.

The Bermuda trip in the summer of 1980 was almost a ritual ending of John's years out of the public eye. Sean would be five that October and would have to go to school, and John would have to get back to his own career. He had been a househusband for long enough. 'This housewife wants a career, too,' he began to joke. At last he had the desire to work again. In Bermuda he took Sean to see the Botanical Gardens and saw an orchid called Double Fantasy. That was all he needed. During the next three weeks he wrote non-stop, mainly in Bermuda while Sean was playing on the beach. Yoko had stayed behind in New York, but she, too, began writing. They were, John explained, to make an album in which they would take alternate tracks. She had demanded equality all the time they had been together. Now she was equal in every way.

In August John booked studio time at the Hit Factory studios in New York and set about hiring a group of session musicians. His contract with EMI/Capitol had expired in 1975 and this time the plan was to pay for the sessions himself and then auction the tapes to the highest and most attractive bidder. The Lennons' own music company Lenono Music would publish the songs. Twenty-four tracks were recorded in a period of about six weeks, of which fourteen were chosen for the come-back album *Double Fantasy*, seven by John and seven by Yoko. The album was intended as a musical conversational piece, but although Yoko's songs were now much more clearly pop-orientated than they had been in the early seventies, John's were the songs that the public really wanted to hear. Yoko understood this, even if John perversely refused to accept it.

John's seven songs on the album were his best work in nearly a decade. Again he was writing from entirely within himself, but with affection and humour. There was none of the anguish of *Walls and Bridges*, none of the radical sloganeering of the early New York days, and none of the sorry-for-himself attitudes of the first couple of solo Lennon records. The only disappointment was that he chose possibly one of the weakest tracks as his come-back single, the 'Elvis/Orbison' rock and roll song, 'Starting Over'.

On 'Cleanup Time' John described succinctly what life had been like for him during his five years as a househusband:

The queen is in the counting home counting out the money,
The king is in the kitchen making bread and honey,
No friends and yet no enemies,
Absolutely free.

None of the hours and hours of interviews he was to do with *Playboy, Newsweek* and the BBC in the next few weeks would express quite so clearly or jocularly as that song the fun he had had at home with his family. If John Lennon had a genius it was in the ability to borrow a line or a rhyme, turn it around and express himself precisely.

The song 'I'm Losing You' might well have been written during the late Beatles period, and the chord changes are similar to 'Glass Onion'. It is a slow, bluesy and lonely song. John Lennon did not have a great singing voice, but it was a voice raw with emotion. When asked why he wrote so personally and if he was not too self-indulgent, John would reply that he might just as easily have put his persona into the third person, and given it a name like Tommy or Ziggy Stardust. Then he would not have been accused of self-indulgence. But he was never one to duck a chance of being criticized.

Possibly the best line in any song that John Lennon ever wrote was contained in 'Beautiful Boy', his love song to Sean:

'Life is what happens to you while you're busy making other plans.'

'Watching the Wheels' was an explanation to all those who had wondered exactly what he thought he was playing at during his years out of the public limelight. Again, he never used two words where one was sufficient. His writing was as clear and uncluttered as it had ever been. The other two songs on the album were both about Yoko, one of which, 'Dear Yoko', used the Buddy Holly introduction from 'Rave On', one of the songs he had sung in The Cavern twenty years earlier, while 'Woman' was simply a song of gratitude.

When the tapes were finished, most of the New York record companies were ready to come in with big offers. Word of mouth from the session musicians was saying that Lennon was back in top form.

The lucky bidder turned out to be David Geffen who had once run Asylum Records and was now setting up his own company, Geffen Records, with a distribution deal with Warner Brothers. On a chance, he sent the Lennons a telegram expressing his interest and was astonished to receive a message the next day from Yoko. A few days later she interviewed him in her office. She told him what she wanted for the rights to the record. He agreed. All that was left now was for Yoko to check his numbers. She checked everyone's numbers, age, date of birth, starsign, etc. to see if they were positive. They were good for Geffen. He was accepted, although he still hadn't asked to hear the tapes. 'If you had asked to hear the music before you wanted to make the deal we wouldn't have gone with you,' she told him. He had probably guessed that.

In their own way the Lennons were playing a game with Geffen. Yoko did the straight, poker-faced bit, and then finally, when the business had been done, Geffen was allowed to meet John. That was the way Yoko worked. She tried to intimidate. When John was around, clowning about, letting his enthusiasm show, no one could be intimidated.

During the autumn months of 1980 John and Yoko continued to work at the Hit Factory, and began to do a series of interviews which were to coincide with the release of the album. Again Yoko ran everything, even going so far as to check to see that the stars were right for interviews.

It was John's dearest wish that he should have a number one record in England. He had been bitterly hurt and angry by the treatment he and Yoko had received from some of the London press in the early seventies, and now he was planning a triumphant homecoming. During the autumn he had even begun to collect old Beatles memorabilia from former employees and friends. He was enjoying talking about Liverpool again, telling his co-producer Jack Douglas how they had made records in his early days.

On Saturday, 6 December he was interviewed by Andy Peebles for the BBC. This was all part of Yoko's campaign to help get John a British number one. John was enjoying himself hugely. The previous day he had done an interview with *Rolling Stone*. He was relishing meeting old friends, and although he didn't know Peebles, he enjoyed a gossip about people he had known at the BBC. It was all like one big reunion. The interview was jokey and good-natured. Afterwards he took Peebles, his producer and Bill Fowler, a representative of the record company, out to dinner at Mr Chow's, breaking his macrobiotic diet which accounted for his emaciated appearance. The jokes never stopped. England was now very much in his mind. Yoko said that he had been talking a great deal about Liverpool recently, and had even begun to choke up at the memories.

On Monday, 8 December, Yoko went to work in the office, John now wanted to see other friends from England, although it was already becoming clear that 'Starting Over' was not likely to reach the top of the charts. When she told John he just shrugged and smiled, and went to get his hair cut, back to the style he had worn it in Hamburg. He was almost back to the way he had looked as a youth. In the afternoon Annie Leibovitz, the *Rolling Stone* photographer, went round to the Dakota to take a front cover picture of John. He chose to be photographed naked, curled up in a foetal position holding on to Yoko and kissing her. He was still on a high of excitement. Yoko had by now arranged another interview with him for the following day. I was to meet them in the afternoon. There were going to be more reunions. In November 'Mercury was in retro' and it had been a bad time to meet, I had been told. Now John was at a peak of excitement and energy.

In the evening John and Yoko went down to the recording studios to remix a disco record that Yoko had made called 'Walking on Thin Ice'. She wanted him to get his number one in England: but he wanted her to have a hit of her own. That night David Geffen popped in to see them. John was, said Geffen, as happy as he had ever seen him.

At ten thirty the mixing of 'Walking on Thin Ice' was completed.

The Lennons had considered going out to eat. Instead they decided to go straight home. Just before eleven o'clock their hired limousine dropped them at the Gothic archway to the Dakota complex. Yoko got out first and walked across into the courtyard, past the doorman and towards the inner gate. As John followed, a few paces behind, he heard someone call his name: 'Mr Lennon.' He turned to see who it was.

I Read the News Today,
Oh Boy . . .

Mark David Chapman was a Beatle fan from childhood. Born in Fort Worth, Texas, in 1955, the year before Elvis Presley was to revolutionize popular music, he grew up in a quiet suburb of Atlanta, Georgia. He was nine when the Beatles first toured America and, like millions of other children, he became totally obsessed with them, eventually joining a group where he could practise playing Beatle riffs. John Lennon was his special hero. He worshipped him.

According to most reports Chapman was a not unlikeable boy, although he had a streak of rebelliousness in him which disturbed his father who had been a sergeant in the air force. For a while Chapman became a Jesus freak, but then, after graduating from high school in 1973, he got a full-time job with the YMCA and was sent to the Lebanon in 1975 as a missionary. When the war there broke out he returned home and was sent to help Vietnamese refugees who were awaiting resettlement at Fort Chaffee, Arkansas.

A year later he decided to go to college, but dropped out after an unhappy college romance and took a job as a security guard in Atlanta, where he was taught how to use a gun. A year later he moved to Hawaii where he had a nervous breakdown and made two unsuccessful attempts at suicide. In June 1979, now working as a security guard in Honolulu, he married a Japanese American girl, Gloria Abe. His interest in Lennon remained obsessive, as was his interest in art.

In October 1980 his obsession turned into delusion. He left his job in Honolulu, signing himself out as John Lennon, and bought himself a .38 calibre revolver for 169 dollars. In early December he turned up outside the Dakota building in New York, watching the comings and goings of the Lennon staff and mixing with the other fans who always hung about there – just as they had been hanging about for seventeen years. In the late afternoon of 8 December he saw his idol, and perhaps in his own mind his other half, leaving the Dakota, and asked John to sign a copy of *Double Fantasy*. As always, John signed. 'They won't believe this in Honolulu,' Chapman is reported to have told another fan.

But when the Lennons returned home that night Chapman was no longer holding the album. In his pockets were several hours of cassettes of Beatle records. In his hand he held his revolver.

When John heard his name called from the shadows Mark Chapman stepped forward, sank down to one knee and, steadying his gun with both hands the way he had been taught, he shot five times at point-blank range into the body of the man he worshipped.

Bleeding profusely, John staggered into the office of the doorman who would have been locking the outer gates at eleven o'clock. 'I'm shot,' he murmured as he sank to the floor. Within minutes the police arrived. Chapman was waiting to be arrested, reading a copy of *The Catcher in the Rye*.

John was lying unconscious while Yoko sobbed over him. He died from massive blood-loss in the back of a police car on the way to Roosevelt Hospital, fifteen blocks away.

'Do you know what you just did?' a police officer asked Chapman.

'Yes. I just shot John Lennon,' came the reply.

'If you stay in this business long enough it will get you in the end,' John used to say about rock and roll. He had always known and been frightened of the hysteria of the fans and the freaks he attracted. But there was nothing he could ever have done to protect himself. He had survived all the demons within: the Beatle hysteria, dope, drink, separation, public hatred and ridicule, and he had emerged at the end of it all still with a joke and a pun and plans for another forty years' work. To millions of people he was a friend. His work was so personal, so open. Mark Chapman's obsession was the result of that openness.

Chapman identified with Lennon as did hundreds of thousands of others. And Chapman's action was the ultimate insanity of fan-mania. He had tried to kill himself on two occasions, and been unsuccessful. So he killed the thing he worshipped, the man he wanted to be, the man he sometimes thought he was.

As an individual Mark Chapman is not important in the story of John Lennon. He was just an unhappy, deranged freak with a gun. John Lennon was killed by his own fame, and by a society he loved, but a society which tolerates medieval laws for the control of weapons. John Lennon was a victim of rock and roll fan lunacy and the gun lobby which makes it possible for pathetic psychopaths to become killers for as little as 169 dollars.

The worldwide contagion of grief which followed the murder would not have pleased him. He did not believe in the cult of the dead hero. He believed in the living. Eight weeks earlier he had told David Sheff of *Playboy*: 'I don't appreciate worship of dead Sid Vicious or of dead James Dean or of John Wayne.' He didn't, he told everyone, believe in yesterday.

But millions of people did believe in just that. News of his death hurtled around a stunned world. In New York even the sacrosanct televised football game was broken into with news of the killing. In England, transatlantic telephone calls broke the sleep of Auntie Mimi and Paul McCartney as Yoko explained what had happened. Cynthia, who was staying with Maureen Starkey, Ringo's former wife, did not find out until the following morning. Immediately Julian, now aged seventeen, flew to New York. Ringo was already there, having flown up from the Bahamas.

Outside the Dakota building thousands of numbed fans began to congregate. Flowers, unable to be delivered to Yoko, were piled high against the iron gates. Radio stations everywhere played the favourite Lennon tracks constantly. In England, 'Starting Over' jumped into number one position in the charts.

Less than two days later John's body was cremated at a private and secret ceremony. Yoko appealed to his fans to pray for him. On Sunday, 14 December, a ten-minute silent vigil was held at Yoko's suggestion. All around the world radio stations went off the air. In Liverpool thousands of fans apparently misunderstood the occasion completely and sang 'She Loves You'. That would have amused John. In Central Park 100,000 people assembled in silence at two o'clock, while above them the television news helicopters chattered. The favourite song in New York was 'Give Peace a Chance'. Later, when the shock was wearing off, cynics would deride the tears which were shed that day. But the cynics did not understand. Those who cried were crying as much for their own lost youth as for the memory of John Lennon.

John's will was simple and straight to the point. His estate was valued at twelve and a half million pounds, not counting the various properties and trust funds which he had set up. Yoko was to receive half, and the rest was to go into trust mainly for Julian and Sean. Typically there was a down to earth Lennon clause to prevent any arguing after his death. If anyone disputed his will, he had instructed, that person was to receive nothing whatsoever.

Yoko went back to work on 19 January. By then she had received nearly two hundred thousand letters from sympathizers. In America, 'Starting Over' and *Double Fantasy* stayed at the top of the charts, while in England EMI had re-released 'Imagine' and 'Happy Christmas (War is Over)', and enjoyed massive hits over the Christmas holiday. Within a month two million records had been sold in Britain alone. By the end of January the single 'Woman' became the third John Lennon number one hit within a month, and the bookshops were filled with magazine tributes. The fan-mania which had turned Mark Chapman into a killer was now turning John Lennon into a saint.

He would have expected it: but he would not have liked it. He was never a saint . . .

Lennon's Recordings

1963

PLEASE PLEASE ME

I Saw Her Standing There; Misery; Anna; Chains; Boys; Ask Me Why; Please Please Me; Love Me Do; P.S. I Love You; Baby It's You; Do You Want To Know A Secret; A Taste Of Honey; There's A Place; Twist And Shout.

WITH THE BEATLES

It Won't Be Long; All I've Got To Do; All My Loving; Don't Bother Me; Little Child; Till There Was You; Please Mr Postman; Roll Over Beethoven; Hold Me Tight; You Really Got A Hold On Me; I Want To Be Your Man; Devil In Her Heart; Not A Second Time; Money.

1964

A HARD DAY'S NIGHT

Hard Day's Night; I Should Have Known Better; If I Fell; I'm Happy Just To Dance With You; And I Love Her; Tell Me Why; Can't Buy Me Love; Any Time At All; I'll Cry Instead; Things We Said Today; When I Get Home; You Can't Do That; I'll Be Back.

BEATLES FOR SALE

No Reply; I'm A Loser; Baby's In Black; Rock And Roll Music; I'll Follow The Sun; Mr Moonlight; Kansas City; Eight Days A Week; Words Of Love; Honey Don't; Every Little Thing; I Don't

Want To Spoil The Party; What You're Doing; Everybody's Trying To Be My Baby.

1965

HELP!

Help!; The Night Before; You've Got To Hide Your Love Away; I Need You; Another Girl; You're Gonna Lose That Girl; Ticket To Ride; Act Naturally; It's Only Love; You Like Me Too Much; Tell Me What You See; I've Just Seen A Face; Yesterday; Dizzy Miss Lizzy.

RUBBER SOUL

Drive My Car; Norwegian Wood; You Won't See Me; Nowhere Man; Think For Yourself; The Word; Michelle; What Goes On; Girl; I'm Looking Through You; In My Life; Wait; If I Need Someone; Run For Your Life.

1966

REVOLVER

Taxman; Eleanor Rigby; I'm Only Sleeping; Love You Too; Here, There And Everywhere; Yellow Submarine; She Said, She Said; Good Day Sunshine; And Your Bird Can Sing; For No One; Doctor Robert; I Want To Tell You; Got To Get You Into My Life; Tomorrow Never Knows.

A COLLECTION OF OLDIES . . .

She Loves You; From Me To You; We Can Work It Out; Help!; Michelle; Yesterday; I Feel Fine; Yellow Submarine; Can't Buy Me Love; Bad Boy; Day Tripper; A Hard Day's Night; Ticket To

Ride; Paperback Writer; Eleanor Rigby; I Want To Hold Your Hand.

1967

SGT PEPPER'S LONELY HEARTS CLUB BAND

Sgt Pepper's Lonely Hearts Club Band; With A Little Help From My Friends; Lucy In The Sky With Diamonds; Getting Better; Fixing A Hole; She's Leaving Home; Being For The Benefit Of Mr Kite; Within You Without You; When I'm Sixty Four; Lovely Rita; Good Morning Good Morning; A Day In The Life.

1968

THE BEATLES (THE WHITE ALBUM)

Back In The USSR; Dear Prudence; Glass Onion; Ob-la-di Ob-la-da; Wild Honey Pie; The Continuing Story Of Bungalow Bill; While My Guitar Gently Weeps; Happiness Is A Warm Gun; Martha My Dear; I'm So Tired; Blackbird; Piggies; Rocky Racoon; Don't Pass Me By; Why Don't We Do It In The Road; I Will; Julia; Birthday; Yer Blues; Mother Nature's Son; Everybody's Got Something To Hide Except Me And My Monkey; Sexy Sadie; Helter Skelter; Long Long Long; Revolution; Honey Pie; Savoy Truffle; Cry Baby Cry; Revolution 9; Goodnight.

UNFINISHED MUSIC NO. 1 – TWO VIRGINS

Two Virgins no. 1; Two Virgins no. 2; Two Virgins no. 3; Two Virgins no. 4; Two Virgins no. 5; Two Virgins no. 6; Hushabye Hushabye; Two Virgins no. 7; Two Virgins no. 8; Two Virgins no. 9; Two Virgins no. 10.

YELLOW SUBMARINE

Yellow Submarine; Only A Northern Song; All Together Now; Hey Bulldog; It's All Too Much; All You Need Is Love.

1969

UNFINISHED MUSIC NO. 2/LIFE WITH THE LIONS

Cambridge, 1969; No Bed For Beatle John; Baby's Heartbeat; Two Minutes; Silence, Radio Play.

ABBEY ROAD

Come Together; Something; Maxwell's Silver Hammer; Oh! Darling; Octopus' Garden; I Want You-She's So Heavy; Here Comes The Sun; Because; You Never Give Me Your Money; Sun King; Mean Mr Mustard; Polythene Pam; She Came In Through The Bathroom Window; Golden Slumbers; Carry That Weight; The End; Her Majesty.

THE WEDDING ALBUM

John And Yoko, Amsterdam.

PLASTIC ONO BAND/LIVE PEACE IN TORONTO

Blue Suede Shoes; Money; Dizzy Miss Lizzy; Yer Blues; Cold Turkey; Give Peace A Chance; Don't Worry Kyoko; John John.

1970

LET IT BE

Two Of Us; Dig A Pony; Across The Universe; I Me Mine; Dig It; Let It Be; Maggie May; I've Got A Feeling; One After 909; The Long And Winding Road; For You Blue; Get Back.

JOHN LENNON/PLASTIC ONO BAND

Mother; Hold On John: I Found Out; Working-class Hero; Isolation; Remember; Love; Well Well Well; Look At Me, God; My Mummy's Dead.

1971

THE EARLY YEARS

Ain't She Sweet; Cry For A Shadow; Let's Dance; My Bonnie; Take Out Some Insurance On Me Baby; What'd I Say; Sweet Georgia Brown; The Saints; Ruby Baby; Why Can't You Love Me Again; Nobody's Child; Ya Ya.

IMAGINE

Imagine; Crippled Inside; Jealous Guy; It's So Hard; I Don't Want To Be A Soldier; Give Me Some Truth; Oh My Love; How Do You Sleep?; How?; Oh Yoko!.

1972

SOME TIME IN NEW YORK CITY

Woman Is The Nigger Of The World; Sisters Of Mercy; Attica State; Born In A Prison; New York City; Sunday Bloody Sunday; The Luck Of The Irish; John Sinclair; Angel; We're All Water;

Cold Turkey; Don't Worry Kyoko; Well (Baby Please Don't Go); Jamrag; Scumbag; Aii.

1973

THE BEATLES 1961 – 1966

Love Me Do; Please Please Me; From Me To You; She Loves You; I Want To Hold Your Hand; All My Loving; Can't Buy Me Love; Hard Day's Night; And I Love Her; Eight Days A Week; I Feel Fine; Ticket To Ride; Yesterday; You've Got To Hide Your Love Away; We Can Work It Out; Day Tripper; Drive My Car; Norwegian Wood; Nowhere Man; Michelle; In My Life; Girl; Paperback Writer; Eleanor Rigby; Yellow Submarine.

THE BEATLES 1967 – 1970

Strawberry Fields Forever; Penny Lane; Sgt Pepper's Lonely Hearts Club Band; With A Little Help From My Friends; Lucy In The Sky With Diamonds; A Day In The Life; All You Need Is Love; I Am The Walrus; Hello Goodbye; The Fool On The Hill; The Magical Mystery Tour; Lady Madonna; Hey Jude; Revolution; Back In The USSR; While My Guitar Gently Weeps; Ob-la-di Ob-la-da; Get Back; Don't Let Me Down; The Ballad Of John And Yoko; Old Brown Shoe; Here Comes The Sun; Come Together; Something; Octopus' Garden; Let It Be; Across The Universe; The Long And Winding Road.

MIND GAMES

Mind Games; Tight Ass; Aisumasen (I'm Sorry); One Day (At A Time); Bring On The Lucie (Freeda People); Nutopian International Anthem; Institution; Out Of The Blue; Only People; I Know (I Know); You Are Here; Meat City.

1974

WALLS AND BRIDGES

Going Down On Love; Whatever Gets You Through The Night; Old Dirt Road; What You Got; Bless You; Scared; No. 9 Dream; Surprise Surprise (Sweet Bird Of Paradox); Steel And Glass; Beef Jerky; Nobody Loves You When You're Down And Out; Ya Ya.

1975

ROCK 'N' ROLL

Be-Bop-A-Lula; Stand By Me; Rip It Up/Ready Teddy; You Can't Catch Me; Ain't That A Shame; Do You Want To Dance; Sweet Sixteen; Slippin' And Slidin'; Peggy Sue; Bring It On Home To Me/Send Me Some Lovin'; Bony Moronie; Ya Ya; Just Because.

SHAVED FISH

Give Peace A Chance; Cold Turkey; Instant Karma; Power To The People; Mother; Woman Is The Nigger Of The World; Imagine; Whatever Gets You Through The Night; Mind Games; No. 9 Dream; Happy Christmas (War Is Over); Give Peace A Chance.

1976

ROCK 'N' ROLL MUSIC

Twist And Shout; I Saw Her Standing There; You Can't Do That; I Want To Be Your Man; I Call Your Name; Boys; Long Tall Sally; Rock 'n' Roll Music; Slow Down; Kansas City; Money (That's What I Want); Bad Boy; Matchbox; Roll Over Beethoven;

Dizzy Miss Lizzy; Any Time At All; Drive My Car; Everybody Is Trying To Be My Baby; The Night Before; I'm Down; Revolution; Back In The USSR; Helter Skelter; Taxman; Got To Get You Into My Life; Hey Bulldog; Birthday; Get Back.

MAGICAL MYSTERY TOUR

Magical Mystery Tour; Fool On The Hill; Flying; Blue Jay Way; Your Mother Should Know; I Am The Walrus; Hello Goodbye; Strawberry Fields Forever; Penny Lane; Baby You're A Rich Man; All You Need Is Love.

1977

THE BEATLES AT THE HOLLYWOOD BOWL

Twist And Shout; She's A Woman; Dizzy Miss Lizzy; Ticket To Ride; Can't Buy Me Love; Things We Said Today; Roll Over Beethoven; Boys; A Hard Day's Night; Help!; All My Loving; She Loves You; Long Tall Sally.

BEATLES BALLADS

Yesterday; Norwegian Wood; Do You Want To Know A Secret; For No One; Michelle; Nowhere Man; You've Got To Hide Your Love Away; Across The Universe; All My Loving; Hey Jude; Something; The Fool On The Hill; Till There Was You; The Long And Winding Road; Here Comes The Sun; Blackbird; And I Love Her; She's Leaving Home; Here, There And Everywhere; Let It Be.

LOVE SONGS

Yesterday; I'll Follow The Sun; I Need You; Girl; In My Life; Words Of Love; Here, There And Everywhere; Something; And I Love Her; If I Fell; I'll Be Back; Tell Me What You See; Yes It Is;

Michelle; It's Only Love; You're Going To Lose That Girl; Every
Little Thing; For No One; She's Leaving Home; The Long And
Winding Road; This Boy; Norwegian Wood; You've Got To Hide
Your Love Away; I Will; P.S. I Love You.

1979

BEATLES RARITIES

Across The Universe; Yes It Is; This Boy; The Inner Light; I'll Get
You; Thank You Girl; *Komm gib mir dein Hand* (I Want To Hold
Your Hand); You Know My Name (Look Up The Number); *Sie
liebt Dich* (She Loves You); Rain; She's A Woman; Matchbox; I
Call Your Name; Bad Boy; Slow Down; I'm Down; Long Tall
Sally.

1980

DOUBLE FANTASY

(Just Like) Starting Over; Every Man Has A Woman Who Loves
Him; Cleanup Time; Give Me Something; I'm Losing You; I'm
Moving On; Beautiful Boy (Darling Boy); Watching The Wheels;
I'm Your Angel; Dear Yoko; Beautiful Boys; Kiss Kiss Kiss;
Woman; Hard Times Are Over.

Index

Index

Index

Index

long live us all y'all,
love to you and yours
from me and mind how you goffer,
I remain
discreetly,
johnandoryoko.

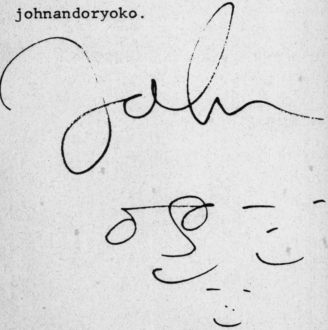